2/24/91

Property
of
A.S. Pinkit *

* better known
as Andy Sjostrom

Special Forces and Missions

Other Publications:

TIME-LIFE LIBRARY OF CURIOUS AND UNUSUAL FACTS
AMERICAN COUNTRY
VOYAGE THROUGH THE UNIVERSE
THE THIRD REICH
THE TIME-LIFE GARDENER'S GUIDE
MYSTERIES OF THE UNKNOWN
TIME FRAME
FIX IT YOURSELF
FITNESS, HEALTH & NUTRITION
SUCCESSFUL PARENTING
HEALTHY HOME COOKING
UNDERSTANDING COMPUTERS
LIBRARY OF NATIONS
THE ENCHANTED WORLD
THE KODAK LIBRARY OF CREATIVE PHOTOGRAPHY
GREAT MEALS IN MINUTES
THE CIVIL WAR
PLANET EARTH
COLLECTOR'S LIBRARY OF THE CIVIL WAR
THE EPIC OF FLIGHT
THE GOOD COOK
WORLD WAR II
HOME REPAIR AND IMPROVEMENT
THE OLD WEST

For information on and a full description of any
of the Time-Life Books series listed above,
please call 1-800-621-7026 or write:
Reader Information
Time-Life Customer Service
P.O. Box C-32068
Richmond, Virginia 23261-2068

THE NEW FACE OF WAR

Special Forces and Missions

BY THE EDITORS OF
TIME-LIFE BOOKS, ALEXANDRIA, VIRGINIA

CONTENTS

For Special Operations: Men a Cut above Others

Bristling with armament, this AC-130H Spectre gunship from the U.S. Air Force 16th Special Operations Squadron delivered air support in Panama during the 1989 invasion. The firepower carried by these converted Lockheed C-130 transports is devastating: two 20-mm Vulcan cannon, a 40-mm Bofors automatic cannon, and a 105-mm howitzer. Television cameras that can see heat sources and structures in low light aid in target acquisition.

Shortly before midnight on December 19, 1989, a cluster of U.S. Navy SEALs assembled at Rodman Naval Base, Panama City, Panama. The name SEAL reflects the ability of these units to infiltrate enemy territory from the sea, through the air, or by land. This night, the superbly conditioned commandos would attack by sea. Within rifle shot across the shipping channel leading to the Panama Canal lay their objective: the *President Porras*, a sixty-five-foot-long patrol boat belonging to the Panamanian Defense Forces. The mission was to disable the vessel.

Crippling the *President Porras* was only one of more than a score of actions planned for American special-operations forces as a prelude to Operation Just Cause, characterized by Washington as a surgical intervention. In attacking Panama, the United States sought to depose Maximum Leader—and alleged drug dealer—Manuel Noriega, thus opening the door for a new civilian government. It would be headed by Guillermo Endaro, who in an election the preceding May had trounced the dictator nearly three to one. Or so it seemed from interviews of voters as they exited the polling places. Only two percent of the votes could be tallied; Noriega had seized most of the ballot boxes and declared the vote null and void. Citing election theft, acts of violence against U.S. military personnel, the need to ensure the safety of the Canal, and indictments issued in Tampa and Miami against Noriega for cocaine trafficking, the United States decided to depose him.

Doing so would require the services of roughly 24,000 U.S. troops, a force calculated to take the fight out of the greater part of Noriega's 15,000-man Panamanian Defense Forces (PDF). About half of the Americans belonged to units that were already stationed in Panama as guardians of the canal. The others were flown in for the occasion from the United States. Slightly more than 4,000 of the total were special-operations troops. They came not only from the SEALs, but from the U.S. Army Rangers and Special Forces. A number of operatives arrived from the Army's low-profile counterterrorist unit—Delta Force. Supported by Blackhawk helicopters from the Army's Task Force 160 and AC-130 gunships *(pages 145-147)* of the Air Force's 919th Special Operations Group, these masters of unconventional warfare had many assignments. Among them, none was more important than apprehending Noriega or, should he elude capture in the opening hours of the operation, preventing his flight from Panama.

The patrol boat *President Porras,* with a top speed of twenty-one knots, offered Noriega a potential avenue of escape that had to be blocked. Although the vessel could have been sunk by naval or aerial gunfire, the last thing the United States wanted at this moment was the unnecessary loss of Panamanian lives, or, on the off chance that the dictator might be aboard the vessel, a dead Noriega for his followers to hold up as a martyr. Four SEALs were heading out in rubber boats from Rodman Naval Base to cripple the patrol boat without casualties to either side. The SEALs were accompanied by four members of a Navy special boat unit—a medic, a coxswain to handle each of the boats, and a mission commander. They would sneak the divers close to the target and pick them up after they had accomplished their mission.

Clad in protective suits of formfitting black spandex, the divers wore closed-circuit breathing apparatus on their chests. The equipment would enable them to spend up to four hours submerged. Moreover, by recirculating and reoxygenating the divers' exhalations, it would release none of the telltale bubbles that ordinary scuba gear emits, greatly reducing the chances of the swimmers' being discovered as they went about their risky assignment. Each two-man team carried a haversack containing a time bomb made from twenty pounds of C-4 plastic explosive, a waterproof clock, a

> **O**ther than the explosives and a sheath knife strapped to a calf, the men carried no weapons.

safety and arming device, and a detonator. To navigate underwater, each pair swam with a "compass board" that had mounted on it not only a compass but a watch and a depth gauge, all of which glowed in the dark. In addition, each swimmer was equipped with a short-range radio in a waterproof bag to use when his head was above water. Other than the explosives and a sheath knife strapped to a leg, the men carried no weapons.

The two raiding craft with the SEALs aboard slipped away from the dock at H-hour minus 1:45, or an hour and forty-five minutes before Operation Just Cause was to commence at 12:45 a.m. on December 20. Originally scheduled for 1:00 a.m., H-hour had only recently been moved forward, an adjustment made because of concern that the large volume of troop movements and air traffic now going on would alert Noriega and his forces to the invasion. The change in schedule came too late for the SEALs to reset the timers on the explosives they carried.

Initially, the raiding craft headed seaward, away from the target, to cross the channel as far away as practical. As a further precaution against discovery, the thirty-five-horsepower outboard motors ran at low speed to reduce noise and leave small wakes not likely to be noticed in the dark. According to the plan for the operation, two U.S. Navy patrol boats, with other SEALs aboard, would soon take up positions in midchannel, ready to rescue the swimmers should Panamanian gunners spot them and begin shooting. Supporting fire would come, if needed, from .50-caliber machine guns, 40-mm rapid-firing cannon, and a grenade launcher aboard the patrol boats—as well as from 60-mm mortars at Rodman.

After crossing the channel in tandem, the boats motored along a mangrove-thicketed shoreline. By H-hour minus 1:15, the lead boat had maneuvered to within 150 yards of the concrete pier where the *President Porras* bobbed, lights ablaze. Taking a compass bearing on the pier, the first two divers slipped over the side into the inky water and began their underwater swim. According to the plan, the second team was to have started swimming for the boat at the same time, but some minutes earlier their engine had conked out. Now the lead craft returned to the disabled boat and towed it beyond the first team's insertion point to make up for the five minutes lost to the engine failure. Taking local currents into account, the men had estimated the number of kicks needed to reach the pier, standard SEALs procedure for gauging distance swum underwater. A differ-

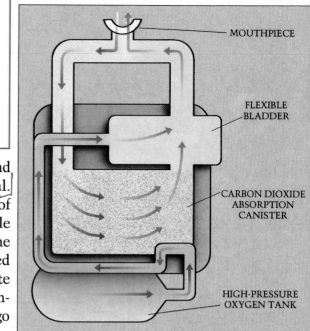

MOUTHPIECE

FLEXIBLE BLADDER

CARBON DIOXIDE ABSORPTION CANISTER

HIGH-PRESSURE OXYGEN TANK

ent starting point for the second team meant that they had to adjust their calculations to avoid overshooting their goal.

Once in the water, the SEALs descended to a depth of about twenty feet and swam directly toward the pier. While one team member navigated with the compass board, the second, gently grasping his buddy's upper arm, counted kicks and served as lookout. If he needed to communicate with the navigator, he could do so silently with a code consisting of squeezes and pauses that signified "surface," "go deeper," "halt," "danger," and "enemy."

Less than a half-hour later, the two pairs of swimmers rendezvoused under the pier to confirm their location, then resubmerged and swam the short remaining distance to the *President Porras*. After surfacing briefly to confirm the identity of the ship, one team hung its explosive haversack from one of the vessel's twin propeller shafts. Then the second team swam under the boat to attach its charge and link the two devices with detonation cord. The blast from either charge would touch off this ropelike explosive, setting off the C-4 in the other satchel. The arrangement ensured that both charges would detonate even if one of the arming devices failed.

Just as the divers were finishing the job, they heard the engine of the *President Porras* start up. Hastily, they swam for an adjacent pier. The uneasy Panamanian crew aboard the vessel, probably reacting to gunfire ashore as H-hour arrived, began tossing hand grenades over the railing. The explosions sent out shock waves, rocking the swimmers and forcing them to take cover behind pilings. As the SEALs swam away, four more explosions shuddered through the water. The swimmers regained their earlier position under the pier, and at precisely one o'clock, a loud noise from the direction of the patrol boat told them that they had done their job well. The swimmers now struck out into the channel for their rendezvous with the rubber boats that had dropped them off earlier. In the meantime, one had towed the other to Rodman Naval Base to have its ailing motor switched for a working one.

Alerted by the blast at the stern of the *President Porras*, alarmed crews on craft anchored nearby cranked up their engines and started their screws turning, a standard defense against underwater swimmers. At the same time, a large oceangoing ship now bore down on the SEALs. To avoid being chewed up by its propeller, they plunged to a depth of forty-five feet, where they waited about ten minutes

To avoid detection as they swim toward a target, Navy SEALs breathe underwater through a closed-circuit apparatus *(diagramed at far left)* that leaves no telltale bubbles. As the diver exhales into his mouthpiece, the air *(red)* is forced into a canister containing a soda-lime mixture that absorbs carbon dioxide. The cleansed air *(blue)* then moves to a flexible bladder, where it mixes with oxygen supplied by a high-pressure tank. The amount of oxygen the diver receives is controlled by a valve that senses the reduction of volume in the bladder as he inhales. The apparatus provides the diver with approximately four hours of oxygen. Because pure oxygen becomes toxic to a diver under pressure of deep water, the SEALs' working depth is limited to forty-five feet.

for the vessel to pass. Then they continued at their customary depth.

Meanwhile, the party aboard the pickup craft sent to the recovery point twelve piers from the patrol boat was growing anxious. Not only had they received no radio transmissions from the SEALs, the swimmers were ten minutes late, and with the invasion finally under way, firefights had broken out ashore. The recovery site, another pier, offered the crews some concealment as tracer bullets whizzed overhead. A quick check of a nearby pier was made, on the chance that the four SEALs had arrived there by mistake. They had not.

To everyone's relief, the first team bobbed up from the blackness at 2:00 a.m., the lenses in their face masks catching the orange glow of fires ignited as the Army battled Noriega's troops. A long five minutes later, the second team surfaced. All told, the SEALs had used three hours and twenty minutes' worth of their four-hour oxygen supply. Not only had they been delayed by the passing ship, but interference caused by the nearby boat engines and other obstacles had blocked radio transmissions and made it impossible for them to report in. Despite these difficulties—minor, as such operations go, yet potentially serious—they had succeeded in eliminating the *President Porras* as a means of escape for Noriega.

Other SEALs were less fortunate that night. Although none lost their lives attempting to disable the remaining vessels of the Panamanian Navy, four died and eight were wounded in an attack on Noriega's private jetliner. It sat chocked at the Punta Paitilla airport, where the Navy men met unexpectedly heavy resistance. Before dawn on December 20, special-ops units altogether would lose ten men killed and ninety-three wounded. More than half the casualties incurred by the Americans in the invasion would be among special-operations forces, a statistic that emphasizes the dangerous nature of their assignments.

Few individuals combine the native intelligence, stamina, self-confidence, and resourcefulness necessary for such work. If there is a single trait that characterizes these modern warriors, it is a ferociously assertive can-do attitude, a belief in their own invincibility. It shines through whether they are asked to help whip a friendly army into shape or to kill the enemy, unhesitatingly, with almost unimaginable violence, often in face-to-face encounters.

In today's world, conflicts between former Cold War adversaries seem far less likely than clashes with opportunists such as Iraqi president Saddam Hussein, who, as the invader of Kuwait, is just one in a rogues' gallery of insurrectionists, guerrillas, zealots, terrorists, kidnappers, and drug lords that circles the globe. Against some of these threats, a few highly trained men of steadfast resolve may accomplish more than all a nation's tanks and infantry to achieve a political goal by force, whether they train others to do the shooting or take direct action themselves.

America has created a smorgasbord of special-ops organizations, all under the umbrella of the United States Special Operations Command (USSOCOM) headquartered at MacDill Air Force Base in Florida. In addition to the Navy's SEALs, there are the Army's Green Berets, Delta Force, and Rangers—as well as units that specialize in psychological operations aimed at persuading an enemy to give up the fight or in putting government bureaucracies back on their feet after a war. Both the Army and the Air Force maintain a fleet of aircraft dedicated to special operations, and even the Marine

Our job is to kill people and destroy things.

Corps has established a quick-reaction, counterterrorist unit. Each has its own planning and training centers, each its particular tasks and responsibilities.

Few such units inspire more admiration than the SEALs. Although their training emphasizes direct action, the members of this select group have diverse roles to play. Operating in close-knit teams, they were among the first to be deployed to the Persian Gulf to help keep Saudi Arabian oil fields out of the clutches of Iraq in the summer of 1990. SEALs can be used for intelligence gathering, ambush, rescues, and reconnaissance in support of amphibious operations. There is even a counterterrorist unit, SEAL Team Six. Any of them can parachute undetected into a hot spot or arrive offshore by surface vessel or submarine. In addition, submarine-borne SEALs have at their disposal Swimmer Delivery Vehicles (SDVs). Capable of transporting as many as six men at a time, these minisubmersibles are used when a swim to a target might prove too exhausting.

The U.S. Army's Special Forces—Green Berets—have a comparably broad repertoire, although their activities are less geared to direct action. Often referred to as "force multipliers," the Green Berets' special talents lie in helping a friendly government field an effective resistance to some threat—an insurgency, for example. In the process, they sometimes confront danger as they lead the troops they have trained.

Of the Army's special-operations units, the Rangers are most primed for high-risk missions. These elite troops—an entire regiment of them—are fighters almost exclusively, trained in such operations as attacking the opponent's command centers, seizing airfields, and cutting roads, railways, and other lines of communications. "Our job," says a former commander of the regiment, "is to kill people and destroy things."

Every major power and many lesser ones have assembled forces with special-operations skills. The Soviets, for example, have Spetsnaz, a word extracted from the Russian phrase *voiska spetsialnogo naznacheniya*—Special-Purpose Forces. Among other activities, Spetsnaz commandos have spearheaded invasions of Hungary, Czechoslovakia, and Afghanistan. And when conventional Soviet infantry tactics failed to find and destroy the elusive mujahedin of Afghanistan, Spetsnaz played an ever-increasing role in the fighting. The British Army has the Special Air Service (SAS), *Air* alluding to the ability to parachute a team into action. Its counterpart in the

13

Royal Marines is the Special Boat Squadron (SBS). Germany, Israel, and North and South Korea all run special-operations forces. Even Denmark, with a population of only four million, supports one of the world's best-trained special-operations forces.

The philosophies underlying such forces stretch between two poles. One pole is embodied by the Spetsnaz. Recruits for these units become the cream of the Soviet Army and Navy. They begin, however, as unseasoned draftees, and few serve more than four years. Their youthfulness—combined with Soviet insistence on utterly unquestioning obedience from the ranks—creates a tough force of special-operations shock troops sometimes likened to the U.S. Army's Rangers.

At the opposite pole stands the 22d Special Air Service Regiment. Illustrious during World War II, the SAS was disbanded immediately following the war but was resurrected during the early 1950s, when Great Britain, still the possessor of a substantial empire, saw that a small force of crack troops might very well minimize the economic and political costs of applying military power in far-off places.

Compared with Spetsnaz troops, SAS men are almost old. Few have less than two years of army experience, and some have many more. A former member may even be available for a special assignment well into his fifties. Moreover, the commandos are chosen not only for physical stamina but for the resourcefulness under stress that enables some men to press onward when others might fade. Mental stability is equally important. The service needs extraordinarily lethal fighters, not psychopathic killers.

The SAS has an "almost insolent certainty about being on top of the job," wrote one British admirer. The attitude is expressed in its motto: Who Dares Wins. Such spirit can turn apparent disaster into success. There are many examples. Once, during parachute training, the sergeant in charge of a practice jump looked on as one of the

Great Britain's Example

Beginning in 1950 and continuing until the end of the decade, British Special Air Service teams waged a largely hidden war against Communist insurgents in Malaya. The four-man SAS patrols worked closely with the Malayan people *(below)* and remained in the bush for extended periods, setting ambushes, sending valuable intelligence to British Army headquarters, and denying free use of the jungles to the Communists.

Impressed by the British example, the United States Army adopted many SAS techniques when it established its own Green Berets Special Forces in Vietnam. But since the Green Berets' initial assignment was largely educational and advisory, the Americans used field units of twelve men, a size that was better suited to teaching indigenous forces a variety of fighting skills.

chutists heaved himself out of the airplane. The chutist's static line—a strong lanyard that opens the parachute a safe distance from the aircraft—became entangled in the tail. Instead of floating to earth under his canopy, the hapless parachutist was violently buffeted by the aircraft's slipstream. Unless something was done, the man might perish—or the plane could crash. The quick-thinking sergeant descended the line, cut the stunned and disoriented man free, then held on to him as they fell. Safely away from the airplane, the sergeant released the auxiliary parachute strapped to the man's chest as backup to the main chute. Finally, with only seconds to spare, he pulled his own rip cord. Both men landed safely.

Translated to the battlefield, boldness and competence of this order have enabled the SAS to succeed where others might well have failed. Among other accomplishments, they helped defeat a burgeoning Communist insurgency in Malaya during the mid-1950s. Twice they have assisted in putting down rebels who threatened the sultan of Oman. And in 1981, a three-man team was largely responsible for undoing a coup d'état in Gambia *(Chapter 3)*.

In SAS's view, an inferior soldier is a weak link, something the service can ill afford. To find men who fit the mold, the regiment has developed a yearlong evaluation process. The test begins with a challenge only the fit can meet: a one-and-a-half-mile run in heavy boots, to be completed in twelve minutes. Those who finish within the allotted time embark on a ten-day trial by ordeal that tests the ability of men to function at the limits of endurance. The torments include ever-lengthening cross-country treks, progressively heavier packs, and little sleep—which is irregularly scheduled and sometimes whimsically denied. The regime, wrote a former SAS member, was "all designed to break down our natural defenses, to take us to the edge of exhaustion and rebellion, to the point where our true characters would come through."

As the exercise unfolds, volunteers are evaluated on their ability to function effectively. In the context of the test, this means reading a map correctly, getting to a destination at the appointed hour, and in general, focusing less on their misery than on the mission at hand. In actual combat, SAS teams can expect to find themselves in situations at least as demoralizing, and they will be deep in enemy territory in the bargain.

After passing initial muster, an SAS recruit can look forward to month after month of grueling field exercises alternating with intensive training in every kind of weapon and equipment imaginable: silenced .22-caliber pistols for killing sentries, all manner of grappling and rappelling gear for climbing up and down buildings, and thermal imaging devices that can detect the presence of humans through walls—to name just a few. Only about 20 percent of the volunteers reach the end of the course. Some have failed, it is said, on the very last day of the fifty-two weeks. Indeed, not until a second year has passed and a man has proved himself again and again in a variety of demanding and stressful situations is he finally considered to be a full-fledged member of the regiment.

The SAS's standards for picking its soldiers have remained virtually unchanged since the unit's revitalization following the war. Furthermore, the spirit behind their selection and training system has greatly influenced other nations. Nowhere is this truer than in the United States.

The ascendance of U.S. special-operations forces in the postwar period began in 1952, after the Army got the upper hand in a squabble with the Central Intelligence Agency (CIA) over who would rebuild America's capabilities for unconventional warfare. The result was a unit made up in part of East Europeans who had escaped the Communist yoke and, it was reasoned, would willingly conduct guerrilla warfare in their homelands should the need arise. These men could join the Army because of a special measure, the Lodge Bill, passed by Congress a couple of years earlier. As a reward, they would receive U.S. citizenship. The architects of this Army unit, which would evolve into the Special Forces, envisioned a regiment consisting of around 2,500 men, half of them East Europeans. Their mission would be "to infiltrate by air, sea, or land deep into enemy-controlled territory and to stay, organize, train, control, and direct indigenous personnel in the conduct of Special Forces operations."

But the American military establishment had doubts, preferring to perform any special operations with a force assembled from conventional units. At a disadvantage in the annual contest for a fair share of the Army budget, the Special Forces, headquartered at Fort Bragg, North Carolina, was something of an orphan. Commanders of other units, reluctant to surrender their best soldiers, sometimes became recalcitrant when the Special Forces sought recruits.

With a speech by President John F. Kennedy, all that began to

Only about 20 percent of the volunteers reach the end of the course.

change. "We need," he told Congress in 1961, "a greater ability to deal with guerrilla forces, insurrection, and subversion, and we must help train local forces to be equally effective." When such words failed to produce results in Washington quickly enough for him, the president took to writing memos to the heads of the military, urging immediate action.

Thus prodded, the Navy took steps to turn the frogmen of its Underwater Demolition Teams (UDTs) into SEALs. The Air Force reestablished the Air Commandos, aviators trained primarily to instruct foreign air forces. The Army showed renewed interest in the special-operations units it already had—the Rangers and the Special Forces. In particular, the Special Forces seized Kennedy's imagination. He doubled the unit's authorized strength to 5,000, focused its mission on combating guerrilla insurgencies, and authorized a jaunty green beret as official headgear. To this mark of distinction the men sewed the unit patch bearing the motto *De Oppresso Liber*—"To Free from Oppression."

Already brewing in Vietnam, a country most Americans had not yet even heard of, was the kind of conflict that Kennedy had foreseen for the Green Berets. In a speech at West Point in 1962, he described it as war "new in its intensity, ancient in its origin—war by guerrillas, subversives, insurgents, assassins; war by ambush instead of combat; by infiltration instead of aggression, seeking victory by eroding and exhausting the enemy instead of engaging him."

The United States had maintained a small military presence in Southeast Asia since 1950, when the U.S. Military Assistance Advisory Group Indochina, headquartered in Saigon, began training South Vietnamese armed forces. Then, in 1957, a Special Forces A-team was sent from Okinawa to join this effort, the first of forty-eight such units eventually sent to Vietnam.

An A-team consisted of a dozen men. Two officers, a captain and a lieutenant, were in charge. A master sergeant—usually the most seasoned member of the team—headed a contingent of enlisted men comprising an intelligence specialist, two medics, two radio men, and two demolition experts. The eleventh and twelfth men—one skilled with individual weapons such as rifles, pistols, and hand grenades, and another with crew-served weapons such as machine guns and mortars—trained the South Vietnamese recruits in arms.

Team members had to be, in the words of one captain, "tough enough to take on 50, trained enough to teach 1,500."

By the early 1960s, the training effort had changed emphasis from helping South Vietnam repel an invasion from the Communist North to dealing with the Vietcong, a guerrilla organization backed by Hanoi. Even a crack army could not anticipate every VC depredation. Vietnam needed a populace that could defend itself. As American involvement in the conflict surged during Kennedy's administration, additional Green Beret force multipliers were dispatched to Vietnam. Their assignment: to turn civilians—chiefly rice farmers in the Mekong Delta and highlanders living in the mountains bordering Laos in central Vietnam—into armed units capable not only of looking out for themselves but of hindering the Vietcong in their largely successful efforts to wrest control of these areas from the South Vietnamese government in Saigon. As the war progressed, the Green Berets would be called upon to perform many other vital tasks, including reconnaissance and strike missions, but as things turned out, there was no job in Vietnam more difficult, lonely, frustrating, or dangerous than tutoring these ragtag bands of citizen soldiers. This venture was called the Civilian Irregular Defense Group (CIDG) program.

Upon being sent to an area to organize a resistance, an A-team would first establish a camp and fortify it with bunkers and trenches. Having provided for their own security, they set about their work. Blistering days, chill nights, frequent bouts of malaria, hepatitis, and dysentery, and the isolation of their outposts would have discouraged all but the most dedicated from the real job—gaining the confidence of the villagers. Toward that goal, the Green Berets had been trained in the rudiments of the local language and customs before departing the United States. Even so, there remained substantial cultural differences to deal with. Montagnard tribesmen of the central highlands bordering Laos and Cambodia, for example, still wore loincloths and hunted with spears and crossbows.

Yet the A-teams—by partaking of the local diet and participating in village festivals, by offering medical care where none had existed, and by being genuinely helpful—enjoyed great success. After one year in the highlands, for example, they had set up twenty-six camps and had armed more than 30,000 men, including 6,000 full-time soldiers and 19,000 part-time militiamen for village defense. With these accomplishments among the Montagnards serving as a model, Special Forces established camps in other parts of South Vietnam among ethnic groups as varied as the Nungs (tribesmen of Chinese extraction living in the mountains) and Khmers (Cambodians who had been born and raised in Vietnam along the border).

The South Vietnamese government seemed to take an ever-dimmer view of the program as it expanded, inasmuch as it turned long-subjugated minorities, discriminated against and abused by those of Vietnamese descent, into effective fighting forces that would be harder to control if the war were ever won. In an effort that seemed calculated to thwart the Green Berets, Saigon took to dumping on Special Forces camps an unsavory collection of jailbirds—violent types, thugs, and army deserters. Not to be defeated, the Americans molded this ragtag collection into competent guerrillas.

Crooks or solid citizens, highlanders or lowlanders, Cambodian, Chinese, or Laotian, the irregulars trained by the U.S. Special Forces constituted a lethal threat to enemy troops entering South Vietnam.

In March 1963, Captain Rod Paschall, officer in charge of an A-team assigned to Darlac province that year, took his medical sergeant and twenty-six Montagnards to attack a rest stop on a forest trail used by the VC as an infiltration route. Paschall and a few of his men had discovered the half-dozen bamboo huts constituting the way station a few days earlier on a reconnaissance patrol near the Cambodian border. On that occasion, warm coals from a doused fire indicated that the occupants had departed only a short time earlier.

The raiding party sneaked out of camp well before dawn to escape notice by Vietnamese living nearby who might be VC informants. Upon reaching the environs of the way station, Paschall established an observation post (OP) to keep an eye on activity there and concealed the rest of his men a short distance away.

On the second afternoon, a Montagnard manning the OP reported that ten enemy soldiers were preparing to spend the night at the target. Thinking themselves safe from attack, the travelers posted no guards, and Paschall's force was

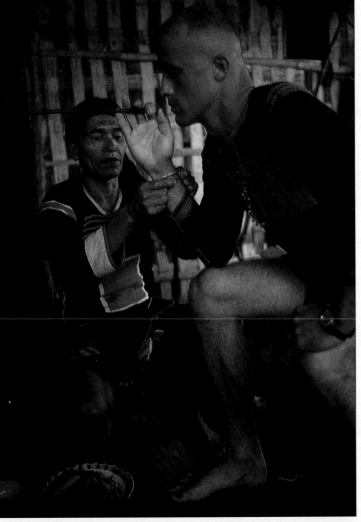

In a ceremony lasting more than two hours, Special Forces team leader Captain Vernon Gillespie receives a ceremonial Montagnard bracelet from a Rhade tribal sorcerer in Vietnam. A token of loyalty, the bracelet symbolically bound together the American and the tribe.

19

The Art of Defense

A fortified village in Vietnam, Buon Brieng was one of a number of settlements that served as defensive outposts against Communist forces in what was known as the Civilian Irregular Defense Group (CIDG) program. The positions were manned by local volunteers, often supported by U.S. Special Forces troops.

Like many of the other fortified communities, Buon Brieng had a formidable set of defenses. Mortars, fired from pits *(detail, center, at right),* covered the camp's outermost areas. Machine guns in bunkers *(far right)* provided interlocking fire to protect both the perimeter and a system of barbed wire barriers. Ringing the edge of the camp was a trench, dug in a zigzag pattern to a depth of five feet, that connected fighting positions and bunkers *(near right).* Cleared fields of fire surrounded the entire position. The Special Forces compound, bordered by a low wall, lay between helicopter landing zones *(white crosses)* and an airstrip *(top center).*

Many camps in the CIDG program added an ancient defense to the modern ones—sharpened bamboo "punji stakes" *(small picture)* implanted in ditches and earthworks to impale unwary attackers.

able to approach within ten yards of the huts before being noticed. All the VC troops might have been captured had one of them not reached for his AK-47 assault rifle. As soon as the Montagnards began shooting, Paschall started yelling, "Cease fire." In seconds, the action was over. Nine of the enemy lay dead, and one had been captured. None of the Montagnards was injured. Paschall detailed half his men to bury the dead well away from the rest stop; the others collected spent cartridge shells and wiped away their tracks with brush. With no evidence of a fight, it would appear to the VC that ten men had vanished without a trace.

Several times during the following months, Paschall led patrols to the same rest stop with similar results. Repeated successes like these made Special Forces troops and camps important targets for the VC. Although the remote outposts were often well fortified, defending one of them could be a harrowing experience. In 1966, the North Vietnamese Army (NVA) was building up its forces near a Special Forces camp opened three years earlier at A Shau, in the northwestern corner of South Vietnam. Sited in a misty, jungled valley between mountains looming 5,000 feet high, the camp was an excellent place to keep an eye on enemy troops and supplies entering northern South Vietnam from Laos.

ince its inauguration, it had grown to include several rusting metal buildings. Its complement of noncombatants included seven interpreters, as well as fifty or so Vietnamese civilians, mostly the families of CIDG members. The camp—Captain John Blair commanding—was defended by seventeen Green Berets, half a dozen troops of the LLDB (Vietnam's special forces), and three CIDG companies comprising 210 men. Among the CIDG were a sprinkling of convicts sent to A Shau as punishment. One of the three CIDG companies was suspected of being riddled with VC. There was also a Mobile Strike "Mike" Force company of 143 Nungs. Blair had requested them as reinforcements after he learned from a captured NVA soldier that an attack was imminent. The Nungs—who loathed all Vietnamese, especially Communists—were fierce fighters. From these mercenaries of Chinese descent and others, the Special Forces in Vietnam had formed the Mike Force, quick-reaction teams that could be sent to places like A Shau in a crisis. Defenses at A Shau consisted of muddy, eroded trenches ringed by rusty barbed wire overgrown by elephant grass. A berm of earth from excavating the trenches formed a low wall around the camp that offered cover from incoming rifle and machine-gun fire.

Captain Blair put the camp on general alert the evening of March 8. In the darkness after midnight, guards could hear noises at the wire that sounded like the North Vietnamese preparing for an assault. To dissuade them, Blair ordered grenade and mortar fire in that direction. The noises ceased.

Shortly before 4:00 a.m., however, NVA mortar shells began to rain down, demolishing buildings and temporarily cutting off communications with the outside world. One Green Beret was killed by a direct hit. Another blast severed both legs of senior medic Sergeant Billie Hall. Though gravely injured, he continued to give instructions for treating the wounded until unconsciousness overtook him. He died soon thereafter.

The mortar bombardment continued without pause for forty minutes. Then at 4:30 a.m., NVA troops stormed the camp from the south, where the CIDG force stood entrenched, ready to repel them. Slowed by the barbed wire and underbrush, they were easy targets for withering rifle and machine-gun fire and for mortar rounds that were launched almost straight up from the center of the camp to fall along the wire. The attackers faltered briefly, then re-formed and charged. Again, they were badly cut up by the defenders and broke off the assault. By this time, dawn was approaching.

With too few men to pursue the enemy, the defenders had one hope—air strikes that might drive them off. Low clouds scudding barely 500 feet above the valley floor made it a faint hope at best. As mortar rounds continued to fall on the camp, an AC-47 gunship slipped under the overcast to attack NVA mortars. Essentially a Douglas DC-3 with rapid-firing machine guns pointing out the left side, this plane usually wheeled around its target at an altitude of several thousand feet. At less than 500 feet, it was easily brought down by NVA machine guns. Three of the six crew members died; the others were rescued by one of several helicopters—gunships and observation craft—that appeared on the scene during the day.

Next, A-1E Skyraiders—piston-engine fighter-bombers of World War II vintage—from an Air Commando squadron based 200 miles away at Pleiku dropped through the clouds, which by now had lifted to 800 feet. Piloted by volunteers, they flew the length of the valley, then turned and reversed their course, all the while dropping 250-pound bombs and raking enemy positions with 20-mm cannon fire. To deal with this eventuality, the NVA had positioned 37-mm

All the VC troops might have been captured had one of them not reached for his AK-47 assault rifle.

23

Flames light up the night sky as the CIDG camp at Bu Dop comes under attack in 1965. The Vietcong planned such attacks meticulously. Spies performed detailed reconnaissance, often actually pacing off the distances between command posts, gun positions, and perimeter defenses. The information was then included in maps such as the one below—prepared for the Bu Dop assault and retrieved from the body of a Vietcong several years later.

antiaircraft cannon on the hillsides so that they could shoot down at the A-1s. One pilot likened his experience at A Shau to "flying inside Yankee Stadium with people in the stands firing at you."

At the camp, ammunition and medical supplies were running low. Two C-123 cargo planes had been dispatched to replenish the camp by parachute. Upon arrival, however, they could not see the camp for the clouds. Major Bernard Fisher, an A-1 pilot on the scene, guided the C-123s right to the camp, but because the supplies were dropped through the overcast, some of the parachutes drifted beyond the perimeter. A few brave souls, sneaking through the elephant grass, managed to retrieve some of the boxes, even though every movement seemed to draw rifle or machine-gun fire from the North Vietnamese, who were forming for another assault.

Just then more air support arrived—this time in the form of two B-57 Canberra bombers, twin-engine early-1950s-vintage jet bombers. Led through a hole in the clouds by Fisher in his A-1, the planes swept in to bomb the assembling North Vietnamese. The Canberras attacked with CBUs (Cluster Bomb Units), canisters of golf-ball-size antipersonnel bomblets that explode near the ground. Popping open after leaving the plane, the canister scatters dozens of the bomblets over a wide area. The effect of a direct hit on troops in the open is devastating; the NVA battalion was decimated. Observers on the ground credited the A-1s and B-57s with killing as many as 500 of the enemy. Just before dark, Fisher escorted a helicopter into the camp to evacuate wounded as another night of anxiety began.

At 4:00 a.m., the enemy repeated the mortar attack of the preceding night, obliterating almost all of the camp's remaining structures. Then, an hour later, a wave of North Vietnamese came rolling toward the camp, again from the south. At this point, the CIDG company suspected of being wormy with VC showed its true colors by joining the enemy in their attack. The NVA poured into the compound, where chaos reigned for three hours as the remaining defenders fought off their assailants in face-to-face shootouts and grappled with them in gouging, punching, slashing hand-to-hand combat. Heroic though their actions were, the men were backed toward the north wall and the concrete communications bunker. Making a stand there, they were able to knock back a charge.

Meanwhile, two Green Beret sergeants had rallied their surviving Nung riflemen and counterattacked the NVA that had swarmed into the camp, but a hail of automatic weapons fire mowed down the Nungs. In desperation, Blair had aircraft strafe and bomb the camp. But it soon became apparent that there was no chance of hanging on any longer. The captain radioed for a helicopter evacuation, and the survivors retreated northward to await rescue. By this time, fewer than half the original garrison were left alive, and many had been wounded. Some climbed over the wall, while a few valiant souls remained inside the camp to keep the NVA at bay.

Major Fisher, meanwhile, had returned with several other A-1s to do as much damage to the enemy as they could. Two Skyraiders were shot down. The pilot of one died when his aircraft crashed into a mountainside, but the pilot of the other, Major Stafford Myers, managed to land his burning plane on the A Shau airstrip. Uninjured, he leaped from the cockpit, scrambled down the wing, and took cover alongside the runway. Overhead, Fisher saw that Myers could not possibly reach the dubious safety of the camp, so he decided to set down and pick him up. "I knew it wasn't wise," he later recalled, "but it was one of those situations you get into. You don't want to do it, but you've got to, because he's part of the family, one of our people. You know you have to get him out of there."

Covered by his own wing man and Myers's, Fisher landed. Dodging debris that littered the runway, he taxied to where he had seen Myers, who began sprinting for the plane. He reached the aircraft just as Fisher looked down from the cockpit to see "two little red, beady eyes trying to crawl up on the back of the wing." Fisher reached down, grabbed Myers by the seat of the pants, pulled him headfirst into the cockpit, then took off for home. Major Fisher's heroism earned him the Medal of Honor.

Sixteen Marine UH-34 choppers, capable of carrying a dozen or more men, answered Blair's call for help. They were escorted by half a dozen UH-1B Huey gunships and a brace of A-1s. As the first helicopter touched down, the lieutenant in charge of the Vietnamese special forces at A Shau rose up. He and most of his men had behaved badly during the fighting, hiding through most of it. Now he sprinted toward the craft, his cohorts close behind. This cowardly act started a stampede. In a mad rush, the Vietnamese CIDG panicked, dropped their weapons, then trod on their own wounded to get aboard. The injured who could marshal the strength and withstand the pain of moving began to crawl and stumble toward the arriving helicopters. In an effort to restore order and keep the craft from being swamped, Green Berets and helicopter crewmen fired on the rabble, killing several and driving back the rest. Then as the heavily burdened choppers took off, the North Vietnamese aimed their fire at them, knocking the tail rotor off the first craft and causing it to crash. The crew dragged the casualties back to the landing zone (LZ) and joined the beleaguered soldiers they had been attempting to evacuate. In the end, only six other helicopters were able to land. Together, they evacuated not even seventy men.

A handful of Green Berets now dashed from the communications bunker toward the LZ. When they arrived, every man wounded by NVA gunfire, no evacuation helicopters remained. Fortunately, one of the Huey gunships still on the scene spotted one man as he staggered onto the LZ, both his arms smashed and a gaping hole torn in his chest. The Huey descended and picked up the battered group.

With night falling, the rescue effort was suspended, leaving nearly 150 men stranded. In two groups, they set off cross-country in the dark. All night they fought a rearguard action as enemy patrols tried to intercept them. The next morning, helicopters renewing the evacuation effort picked them up in different places several kilometers from the camp.

Special Forces abandoned the A Shau site permanently, deeming it indefensible, and the North Vietnamese themselves did not stay on. A week or so later, a handful of Americans returned on a body-recovery mission. They found 200 of the dead lying about in the grass that had sprouted between shell holes filled with muddy water. Bony fingers still clutched .45-caliber pistols. Battery-operated watches on fleshless wrists still counted off the passing hours.

Hunkered down for the night in border outposts like the one at A Shau, Green Berets were on the defensive. However, as long as such bases remained tenable, they served as launch points for reconnaissance missions intended to find out where the enemy was and in what strength. Where evidence of hostile activity was found, a nighttime ambush might be set up and the trap sprung on unsuspecting NVA soldiers who stumbled into the kill zone.

Among the most dangerous of these assignments were those that penetrated deep into enemy-held territory. Typically, such a mission lasted about five days. That was about as long as the food a man could carry—including cooked rice stuffed into clean socks tied

together at the tops and suspended sausage-
fashion around the neck—would hold out. The
patrol generally consisted of two or three Green
Berets and perhaps ten men they had trained. The
team would be inserted by helicopter as close to
the target area as possible. Usually, the chopper
bracketed the real insertion with several fake
ones to conceal the team's location.

On the ground, the men would immediately
form a defensive perimeter and wait in silence
after the noise of the helicopter had faded, ears
cocked for the slightest tip-off to a hostile presence—a cracking branch, perhaps, or a rustle of
elephant grass out of sync with the breeze. Only
when they felt moderately certain that the nearby
jungle did not conceal any of the foe would they
move out, with a point man in the lead and two
or three men as "tail gunner" in the rear. In the
thickest jungle, progress was slow. A day's slog,
interrupted by frequent "listen halts" to see if the team was being
trailed, might cover only a mile or so. Often just one man at a time
would advance. He would then freeze and wait for the second to
move forward, then the second would wait while the third came up,
and so on. If anyone made a sound, the whole party would halt in
its tracks until reassuring silence again permitted motion. Smok-
ing, cooking, and the use of soap were all forbidden, for no other
reason than that the enemy possessed a keen sense of smell.

To spend the night safely among the enemy, a degree of craftiness
was necessary. For example, the patrol leader would often choose
two campsites several hundred yards apart. At one site, known as
a RON (for remain overnight), the men would go through the mo-
tions of establishing camp, even sitting down and eating. After dark

By Truck, Foot, and Bike Down the Ho Chi Minh Trail

Snaking its way from North Vietnam through Laos and Cambodia to key entry points on the borders of South Vietnam, the Ho Chi Minh Trail brought troop reinforcements, supplies, weapons, and ammunition to both the Vietcong and the North Vietnamese Army units operating in the south. An unmarked and ever-shifting system of footpaths, bicycle trails, and roads, the network was hard to detect from the air and impossible to knock out on the ground. Depending on the terrain, the lifeline for the Communists was, as one Green Beret put it, "sometimes a highway. Next a foot trail. Next a bicycle path."

North Vietnamese truckdrivers transported their supplies as far as they could, often along winding mountain roads *(far left)*. Carriers then off-loaded the trucks, packed the goods in homemade rucksacks, and lugged the equipment down the trail on their backs—or on bicycles rigged with a steering yoke across the handlebars. These bicycles, which were pushed, carried loads far heavier than a single man could bear. When steep terrain was encountered, steps were built into the sides of the mountains or latticework ladders were constructed from tree limbs or bamboo *(center)*. Streams were crossed at low-water fording points *(left)* to compensate for the lack of bridges.

North Vietnam

● Hanoi

Gulf of Tonkin

Hainan

Laos

Thailand

Cambodia

South Vietnam

Saigon ●

Gulf of Thailand

they would booby-trap the campsite with claymore mines. This crescent-shaped, antipersonnel weapon stood on metal legs pushed into the ground and could be fired manually or rigged with a trip-wire of fine fishing line. When detonated, it blasted hundreds of steel pellets toward the enemy in a sixty-degree arc of mayhem.

After preparing the first site, the men would sneak away to the second, where they would post watch and sleep within a protective ring of additional claymores. Such precautions paid off time and time again. Many a patrol learned that it had been stalked when mines exploding at the first RON awakened them in the night.

Special-operations patrols often had the job of harassing enemy supply columns along the Ho Chi Minh Trail, the Vietcong lifeline that ran out of North Vietnam southward along the Laotian panhandle and into eastern Cambodia. Such "over the fence" missions into Laos posed special hazards. The terrain followed by the Ho Chi Minh Trail was among the most daunting in Southeast Asia—rugged mountains overgrown with triple-canopy jungle, all-but-impenetrable groves of bamboo, or ten-foot-tall curtains of elephant grass. And the area was infested with NVA troops.

Volunteers were never lacking for these hazardous assignments. One Green Beret sergeant who seemed particularly keen to assume such tasks was Fred Zabitosky. On his third yearlong tour of duty in Vietnam, with thirteen such missions behind him, he stepped forward to lead another.

Most of Zabitosky's visits to Laos had begun without incident, but this time he and his nine-man reconnaissance team landed in a hornet's nest. The jungle clearing where they were deposited by helicopter lay within shouting distance of a large force of NVA.

The team had advanced no more than a hundred yards from the landing zone when a lopsided firefight broke out—Zabitosky and his nine against ten times as many North Vietnamese. By radio, Zabitosky summoned two A-1E Skyraiders that were orbiting overhead in case he needed air support. Meanwhile, working on his belly to avoid being hit by bullets zipping overhead, Zabitosky hung a pair of white phosphorus grenades on a claymore mine so that they would go off when the claymore exploded, producing a cloud of white smoke for the A-1 pilots to aim at.

Zabitosky withdrew a hundred yards or so. Then as NVA troops charged toward the team, he blew the claymore. The Skyraiders zoomed in on the smoke and wiped out the first wave of attackers

Working feverishly, Zabitosky jammed the steel legs of another claymore into the ground in front of him.

with napalm. Working feverishly, Zabitosky jammed the steel legs of another claymore into the ground in front of him. Then, slithering to the rear, he uncoiled the wires attached at one end to blasting caps in the top of the mine and at the other to a hand-held battery-powered detonator called a cricket. Taking a position several yards behind the mine, Zabitosky began firing at the second wave of advancing soldiers with his CAR-15 assault rifle, a shortened version of the standard M-16. Then, as the Skyraiders returned and delivered their load of high-explosive bombs, he exploded the mine.

Zabitosky and company now ran to the LZ and radioed for choppers, learning to their dismay that their ride home was being held up by fighting elsewhere. He and his men were in one hell of a fix. As an enemy company attacked the landing zone, Zabitosky moved along his troops' defensive perimeter, coolly directing their fire. Meanwhile, the A-1s repeatedly raked the Vietnamese with 20-mm cannon fire. Throughout the fighting, the nine-man team—none of whom had been wounded—remained intact, turning back twenty-two attacks before the evacuation helicopters arrived. There were four altogether, two of which descended into the clearing. Half the team hopped onto the first chopper, while Zabitosky and the others scrambled aboard the second.

This helicopter had hardly risen above the treetops when it was hit by an NVA rocket-propelled grenade and fell heavily to earth. Thrown out the door and briefly knocked unconscious by the impact, Zabitosky wakened twenty feet from the hulk, now on fire. He first extracted the dazed pilot, then returned to the helicopter for the copilot just as the fuel tanks exploded and tossed both clear of the wreckage. Despite burns, crushed vertebrae, and broken ribs, Zabitosky hoisted the copilot onto his shoulders and dragged the pilot toward a third chopper, which lifted them to safety. Zabitosky's selfless valor earned him the Medal of Honor, one of seventeen awarded to men of the Special Forces during the Vietnam War.

Combat for special-operations troops was often disconcertingly intimate. A Special Forces sergeant (his name is not recorded), veteran of eight or ten patrols along the Ho Chi Minh Trail, told a vivid account of coming face to face with the foe. Getting ready to plant a mine along the trail, the Green Beret found the dirt packed hard from the trucks that had passed by. He began chopping away at it with his knife when his lookout, hidden in the jungle alongside the track, signaled that someone was approaching. The American

A SEAL in the Mekong Delta

In Vietnam, U.S. Navy SEALs held the responsibility for conducting special operations within ten miles or so of any Vietnamese waterway. Concentrated in the southern end of the country, where the Vietcong were strongest, SEALs emphasized direct action—conducting reconnaissance, springing ambushes, and staging raids along the tributaries of the mighty Mekong River. Some of these men participated in Operation Phoenix, a covert program run chiefly by the Central Intelligence Agency. The project's purpose was to identify, capture, and interrogate Vietcong officials in an effort to unravel the fabric of the enemy's political infrastructure. Those suspected of such complicity were often snatched from their beds in the middle of the night.

Mike Beamon, a former SEAL who served in the Mekong Delta, has spoken hauntingly of this role: "My responsibility was to scout in and get us to a village, get us to a particular spot, go in there and get the person out that we wanted."

On such missions, Beamon preferred to travel with his team—which included a Vietnamese "prisoner handler"—through irrigation ditches, even when the water was chest-high, if for no other reason than "if you got shot at, you had water surrounding you, and that tends to slow a bullet down." More often than not, he carried a duckbill shotgun loaded with No. 4 buckshot, pellets about three-sixteenths of an inch in diameter. The weapon took its name from the shape of the muzzle, which was oval rather than circular in order to direct the shot in a horizontal pattern. And he always took along a Navy K-bar knife honed to razor-sharpness.

Beamon dressed in so-called sterile mode. Other than the number 50 stamped on his clothes, he had no identification. Beamon painted his face black and at times wore a black pajama-type shirt, in mimicry of the Vietcong—anything to present a silhouette that would not be readily recognized as that of an American. "I learned how to walk like a Vietcong, move like a Vietcong, think like a Vietcong."

Although he was tall, Beamon conditioned himself to walking small, with slumped shoulders. "There's a certain way you walk through the jungle when you're comfortable with it. It's like a cat who walks and knows where he's going and what he's doing."

Blending in paid off regularly. On one nighttime mission, Beamon and his companions realized that they were being followed. With no cover available, they dropped to the ground. The enemy began shooting toward them, trying to draw return fire that would reveal the SEALs' location. "Our only hope was to make ourselves look like a pile of logs. So we became a pile of logs. It's incredible to explain what you can become, the illusion that you can present to people."

On this occasion, sixteen armed Vietcong

walked toward the men, who lay facing away from the approaching threat. "They walked up really close, with these lamps," Beamon recounted. "You have to concentrate on whether or not they're seeing you. This kind of intensity, like it's the last second of your life. They came right up to us. We were all so well tuned to one another, we shifted our positions, opened fire, and I'll never forget seeing all those bodies flying in the air. They were just arching as we hit them with our weapons."

Approaching a village on a Phoenix mission in the early-morning darkness, Beamon chose to go barefoot. By doing so, he avoided leaving boot prints and making noises. From a spare bandage fastened around his head, he fashioned a gag. He stole up to the victim's hut with a Vietnamese assistant, who waited outside while Beamon slipped through the doorway. Once across the threshold, he stood motionless, alert to any change in the breathing of the slumbering inhabitants.

When he had identified the victim, Beamon shoved the gag into the man's mouth, held the K-bar knife under his throat, then dragged him out of the hut and turned him over to the Vietnamese prisoner handler. Then the team withdrew as silently as they had come.

Beamon had good reason to be proud of his stealth and his instincts for survival, with which he kept not only himself but also his buddies alive during the five months or so they spent in the field together.

But he did not care much for the work. Tension and danger were unrelenting. He and the others swallowed the stimulant dextroamphetamine to keep alert for a mission. He said later, "I'd just turn into a pair of eyeballs and ears." Afterward, a few beers helped him to fall asleep.

While Beamon had no compunctions about kidnapping someone from bed, he disliked having to booby-trap the hut doorway with a hand grenade to cover his escape after an abduction. The likely victims would be innocent members of his target's family. Far more dismaying, however, were those occasions when his captive was dispatched on the spot, as happened on Beamon's very first Phoenix mission. After leading the team back to the boat they had come in, he noticed that the prisoner was missing. When Beamon asked where the man was, the bandage he had fashioned into a gag was returned to him drenched with blood. The man's throat had been slit.

A good idea corrupted, Operation Phoenix was not only marred by assassination but also undermined by quotas and rewards that encouraged the kidnapping of blameless individuals for the sake of reporting a high number of VC officials seized, for the comfort of some extra money, or even for personal revenge. Few would argue today that Operation Phoenix accomplished its aims, and many see it as representing a type of activity that is best not repeated.

dashed into the brush clutching his CAR-15 and saw an NVA sol-dier coming down the road with an AK-47 assault rifle slung over his shoulder. The soldier noticed the loose earth, looked around, "and then he just went at a ninety-degree angle from the trail," said the Green Beret, "right toward me. He never pointed his rifle or nothing, but he walked right up to me. I had my CAR-15 pointed right at his face, no more than a few feet away. He looked at the rifle and he looked at me and he didn't know what to do. I started smiling at him, thinking, 'You are in bad trouble, buddy.' "

But the American did not want to shoot. Had he done so, other North Vietnamese troops would have heard the discharge, and he would not have been able to finish planting the mine. "I just figured," recalled the sergeant, "if he leaves, he leaves. I kind of smiled at him, and he let off a smile, and he backed up, got on the road, and kept on walking. I figured he would try for his weapon, but he didn't." Returning to the road, the American finished burying the mine. Then he melted deeper into the jungle, wondering wheth-er the sentry would report having seen him.

The answer came just around dusk. Enemy trucks could be heard approaching. The mine exploded. The sergeant remembered think-ing: "You didn't tell anybody! Live and let live. He just let it go."

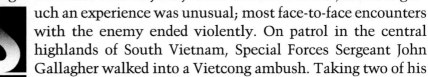uch an experience was unusual; most face-to-face encounters with the enemy ended violently. On patrol in the central highlands of South Vietnam, Special Forces Sergeant John Gallagher walked into a Vietcong ambush. Taking two of his men, he attempted to outflank the hidden assailants and take them out. He later recalled, "I got around to the side and pointed my M-16 at them and this person turned around and just stared, and I froze, because it was a boy. I would say between the ages of twelve and fourteen. When he turned at me and looked, all of sudden he turned the whole body and pointed his automatic weapon at me, I just opened up, fired the whole twenty rounds right into the kid, and he just laid there. I dropped my weapon and cried."

The gun was no less lethal for being in a boy's hands, and hesi-tation in such circumstances might have cost Gallagher his life. Thus, special-ops troops, like others fighting in Vietnam, learned to fire almost reflexively. As one man, a Navy SEAL, put it, "I don't think I made a habit of shooting people unnecessarily, but at the same time my fear level was so high that if it meant me being afraid or them being dead, usually the person was dead."

In addition to quick reflexes, accomplishing a mission in the enemy's backyard often demanded a flair for improvisation. Green Beret Captain James G. "Bo" Gritz displayed both on a visit to the wreckage of a U-2 high-altitude reconnaissance plane that had exploded along the Cambodian border as it returned from a mission over North Vietnam. The pilot ejected safely and was rescued.

Aboard the U-2 was an electronic "black box" that could compromise the aircraft's reconnaissance capabilities. The box had to be retrieved, even though no one knew just where the U-2 had crashed. At best guess, the wreckage had fallen within a 440-square-mile core of Vietcong-dominated territory. "Looking for the plane in that virtually trackless expanse," wrote General William C. Westmoreland, commander of American forces in Vietnam, "would be like looking for a raft in thousands of miles of ocean, or, assuming the black box had blown clear of the plane, like looking for a chip of wood on that same vast sea." Yet this was exactly what Captain Gritz was asked to do.

From Duc Phong Special Forces camp, a base well east of Cambodia, Gritz, the rest of his A-team, and a 150-man force of Cambodian CIDG were ferried to the search area by helicopter as stealthily as was possible. Unfortunately, the whap of the rotor blades alerted the enemy, and shortly after landing, the men found themselves skirmishing with small groups of Vietcong, whom they killed at a cost of several wounded. The casualties forced Gritz to

In a desperate search, Green Beret Captain James G. "Bo" Gritz
(far left, second from right) set
out to find a downed U-2 spy
plane in the Vietnamese jungle.
With little more to go on than a
map outlining a huge expanse of
rugged terrain, Gritz did find the
wreckage of the plane (center)—
but not its top-secret electronic-
countermeasures "black box."
The clue to the missing box finally came from a wounded VC
soldier (near left) captured by
Gritz's team during an ambush.

call for a medevac helicopter, giving the enemy another chance to pinpoint his location.

On the third day of cutting back and forth through the jungle and tall stands of elephant grass in search of the downed U-2, skirmishing with the enemy when unable to avoid them, Gritz and his men found the plane. But a thorough search of the wreckage failed to turn up what they had come for. From the disturbed look of the scene, Gritz concluded that somebody had already rifled the plane for the box. At this point, many men would have given up the quest, a long shot at best. But Gritz was determined to recover that black box.

He and his team set up an ambush on a trail that showed signs of frequent use. He hoped to capture a Vietcong prisoner who might at least have an idea where the box had been taken. Darkness had just begun to fall when six of the enemy came walking toward the hiding men. The Cambodians opened fire, killing four and wounding the two others, who immediately ran into the jungle, leaving a trail of blood. Even though his little force was now compromised, Gritz was determined to turn a negative into a positive. He stayed right where he was with his team, certain that the Vietcong would soon come looking for the bodies. Upon his signal, his men were to fire on the burial detail, leaving unharmed whichever two soldiers happened to be in the lead. Gritz and one of his sergeants planned to take them alive.

That night, ten Vietcong approached the ambush site single file. As planned, Gritz's men began firing their automatic rifles and detonating claymore mines into the enemy troops. In the heat of the engagement, Gritz and his accomplice leaped at their quarry. If anything, Gritz was overzealous in his application of his "zapper," a special billy club supplied by the CIA, and killed his man, but the sergeant made his catch. In a well-planned ambush at night, the troops springing the trap often get away without casualties, and so it was with Gritz's men.

The prisoner, a mere sixteen years old, had been hurt in the fracas. Gritz, who could speak some Vietnamese, led the young man to believe that if his injury were not treated soon, he would die from it. Furthermore, Gritz told the prisoner that he was not worth keeping alive if he could not guide the party to the black box they were looking for. The ruse worked, and next morning the teenager led them to a Vietcong stronghold that was by now fully alert. The boy even suggested to Gritz that he stood a good chance of surprising this base camp by attacking through its unguarded latrine area.

Gritz and his force waited until dusk, when the fading light would let them distinguish any unarmed women and children who might be present and would allow the team to withdraw under cover of darkness. Guns blazing, they entered the camp. The surprised Vietcong dashed for the protective shelter of tunnels and holes dug in the ground. During the ensuing melee, two of Gritz's cohorts made a quick search for the box and found it. Now the party sprinted back into the jungle.

After they had gone some distance in the dark, Gritz ordered a bivouac. It was Christmas Eve, he realized as he glanced at the luminous dial of his watch. He had only just reflected on the thought when rockets and mortars began exploding nearby. The force scattered, but it regrouped at an alternate RON selected earlier. Gritz radioed for a helicopter, which came in the morning and took out the wounded, the prisoner, and the black box. Several days later, after distancing themselves from the dangerous neighborhood of the base camp, the team was extracted by helicopter.

When Gritz got back to Duc Phong, he visited the hospital in search of the informant. There he discovered that the boy had been released; no one had realized that he was a prisoner. "They gave him a CIDG uniform and a carbine," the amazed Gritz reported later, "patted him on the ass, and told him to go back to his unit."

Most things captured by the enemy during the Vietnam War were not worth the trouble to retrieve. The U-2's black box was a notable exception—as were soldiers or airmen who fell into enemy hands. In the South, as prisoners of the Vietcong, they were often caged in squalid conditions. Many died from disease, mistreatment, and malnourishment. Men held in the North, mostly Air Force and Navy pilots shot down on bombing missions, were almost as much abused. Chances to rescue any of these men, wherever they might be held, tapped deep reserves of courage and fortitude among the men—Special Forces troops, as often as not—who made the attempts. Indeed, not long after the United States had begun to pull back gradually from the war in Southeast Asia, some fifty Green Berets would attempt a truly inspired rescue mission, foraying deep into the lion's den of North Vietnam to spring American aviators from a prison camp that lay less than ten leagues from Hanoi. ★

Techniques for Insertion and Extraction

Beginning a special-operations mission unobserved is often crucial to its success. The end of a mission can require a rescue effort if the team encounters superior numbers of the enemy. With good reason, then, special-ops forces have devised a variety of insertion and extraction procedures. Some, such as the delivery and pickup of SEALs by a speeding powerboat *(overleaf)*, are routine. Others, such as an airplane-rescue technique called Skyhook *(pages 50-53)*, are so risky that no one relishes having to use them.

All insertion and extraction methods must be workable at night. Starlight television cameras and infrared viewing systems help aircrews see what they are doing. Night-vision goggles are nearly indispensable both aloft and on the ground. Dim lights are sometimes used to mark parachute drop zones, the path of a rope, or the position of an individual to be retrieved.

There is no fixed way of performing any of the techniques that are explained on the following pages. Airborne and waterborne methods are frequently combined, and equipment can be substituted or modified. As in so many other aspects of special operations, flexibility is the key requirement.

A wet beginning. A Green Beret jumps from a helicopter into the water near an inflatable boat filled with gear, as a teammate cranks up the outboard motor.

Insertion. Holding his face mask in place, a SEAL rolls into the wake of the inflatable craft, as the next man prepares to follow. For a SEAL to roll from boat to inflatable to water takes less than three seconds.

CONDUCTING A BEACH SURVEY

The roll-off calls for SEALs to roll in rapid succession from a speedboat into an inflatable craft and thence into the water. Deposited some twenty-five yards apart, the men briefly tread water. Then, on a prearranged signal from the team leader, they begin to swim toward shore. Taking care not to splash with their swim fins or otherwise betray their presence, they count their kicks as a measure of the distance they have to swim in order to return to the pickup point. They note the depth of the water, the strength of currents, whether the bottom has rocks or other obstructions that would prevent an amphibious landing, and how violently the surf pounds the beach. Before swimming for the pickup point, each member of the team moves ten or twelve yards along the shore in order to examine a different part of the sea bottom on the return trip.

A High-Speed Delivery System for SEALs

The commander of an amphibious task force planning to storm a beach would rely on a SEAL team to find out what his men will encounter as they near the shore. A reef or an underwater obstacle placed by the enemy can rip the bottom out of a landing craft. Too steep a bottom may make it impossible for amphibious tanks and armored personnel carriers to crawl ashore. A violent surf can swamp such vehicles and drown men who are heavily burdened with packs and weapons.

To facilitate reconnaissance of the beach and adjacent waters, the SEALs have developed an insertion technique called the roll-off, in which the team members drop into the water one at a time from an inflatable craft attached to a powerboat traveling at up to eighteen knots. In less than twenty seconds, a six-man team can be positioned perfectly for a swim to the beach. The pickup basically runs the procedure in reverse.

If a look at the sea bottom is not crucial and the team has other work ashore, the roll-off normally is not used. The technique spreads the SEALs dangerously thin, making a concerted defense all but impossible if they are detected.

Arriving with a Whisper

Inherently silent, the parachute offers an excellent means of clandestine entry—except for the noise made by the delivery aircraft. To solve this problem, two jump techniques have been developed to keep the airplane far from the drop zone (DZ). Both depend on jumping from altitudes as high as 30,000 feet. After that point, however, the two approaches differ.

In the high-altitude, low-opening (HALO) method shown on these pages, the parachutist free-falls to the minimum safe altitude before opening his parachute. While this technique makes for a quick insertion, it is suitable only where the aircraft can fly directly over the drop zone. In other circumstances, the high-altitude, high-opening (HAHO) technique is used (*overleaf*).

Special equipment for both kinds of jump consists of insulated clothing, an oxygen supply, a wrist altimeter, and an unusual parachute. It consists of a double-layer canopy shaped like an airfoil, which generates lift to extend the descent.

30,000 FEET

2,500 FEET

High altitude, low opening. Dropping toward a target like a bomb, the parachutist falls at a speed of roughly 200 feet per second. When he has descended to within about 2,500 feet of the ground—a little more than two minutes after leaving the aircraft—the chutist pulls the rip cord and steers toward the landing point.

The free-fall position. To minimize speed and maximize control, the jumper creates as much wind resistance as possible by slightly bending his arms and legs. Subtle adjustments of hand position equalize airflow so that the jumper does not turn, roll over, or enter a spin.

Steering technique. A jumper maneuvers laterally by pulling one arm in toward his head and also moving the leg on the same side closer to his body's centerline. The resulting decrease in drag causes him to move in that direction.

Regaining control. To recover from a spin, possibly caused by air turbulence, the jumper places his arms against his sides. Drag from his feet causes him to fall head-first, stopping the spin. Then the jumper can safely reassume the free-fall position.

A Cross-Country Ride

30,000 FEET

28,000 FEET

Stretching the range. For the best glide ratio—the distance traveled toward the drop zone versus altitude lost—air must flow unhindered between the upper and lower canopy panels. This requires leaving the parachute's steering toggles in the uppermost position.

Maneuvering. For a turn, the jumper pulls down on one of the steering toggles. To steer left *(above)*, he lowers the left toggle. Doing so curls the left side of the canopy downward at the rear and bends the flow of air. The result is a braking force around which the parachute rotates until the toggle is released. Pulling the toggle all the way to waist level results in the tightest possible turn or spiral.

High altitude, high opening. In a HAHO jump, free fall lasts only eight or ten seconds before the jumper opens the chute. Settling to earth at a rate of fifteen to twenty-five feet per second—depending on air density, temperature, and other factors—he can glide as far as fifteen miles cross-country during the seventy-five minutes a flight might last. For shorter distances, he uses a spiral descent, slowing his lateral progress so that he arrives at the drop zone just as he is ready to touch down.

Preparing to land. When he is several hundred feet above the ground, the jumper pays out a fifteen-foot line tethering a bundle containing his weapon and other equipment for the mission. Separating himself from the gear reduces the chances of injury during the landing.

The final approach. To brake for a landing, the jumper pulls on both toggles simultaneously—taking care not to slow too much too soon, lest the parachute lose lift and drop him hard. Typically, a skilled chutist can touch down at walking speed or less and suffer no greater jolt than he might expect from leaping off a chair.

Up and Out by Rope and Rotor

In Vietnam, special-operations units experimented with a variety of techniques for lifting men from jungle clearings that were too small for a helicopter to set down in. Two worked particularly well. Known as SPIE *(left)* and STABO *(right)*, they have become standard procedures for extracting special-ops troops from any spot that precludes a chopper landing—the side of a mountain, a boat, even a treetop. Both methods require a web harness similar to a parachute's. It can be worn into action or carried in a rucksack. In a pinch, a harness can be fashioned of rope.

Developed by the Navy, SPIE (Special Procedures, Insertion/Extraction) is a single-rope technique. It prevents the men from colliding with each other and frees their hands to fire weapons at antagonists on the ground. Moreover, an unconscious member of a team can be hooked up to a SPIE line and snatched to safety.

STABO (Stabilized, Tactical, Airborne Body Operations), a favorite of the Army, uses multiple ropes. Among other advantages, it allows better helicopter control, and the men can more easily engage and disengage from the lines.

A no-hands extraction. Lifting a team of four using SPIE, the pilot of a CH-47 Chinook takes care not to fly forward until he has raised his charges well above any obstacles on the ground. Below, four SEALs on a beach unhook from a SPIE rope. A clip at the top of the harness snaps onto a ring spliced into the rope, which may have as many as eight rings, set at intervals of about five feet.

Arm-in-arm stability. Trailing behind a UH-60 Blackhawk, men extracted by STABO link their elbows and ankles to form a single unit. A safety rope connects the soldiers at the waist to prevent them from drifting apart should they become separated. By stretching out an arm, a man at the end of the row can stop a spin *(below)*. The troop on the left in the picture is counteracting a tendency for the group to turn clockwise.

Plucked from the Brine by Chinook

An inflatable rubber boat is ideal for clandestine missions where special-operations troops are required to approach from the sea. With its outboard motor muffled by a jacket of rubber insulation, such a craft makes little noise, yet it can reach speeds of about twenty knots. Because its fuel supply is limited, however, the boat must be transported as close to the objective as enemy radar and other defensive measures permit—usually to a point no more than twenty-five to thirty-five nautical miles offshore. Often a ship is used for this purpose, but a helicopter can drop off and pick up the inflatable more quickly.

The Chinook is well suited to this role. The powerful chopper can ship as much as a thousand gallons of water as it dips to the sea's surface and still be able to take off. Moreover, the aircraft's raised flight deck prevents water from sloshing forward into the cockpit area.

The boat is carried to the drop-off point fully inflated. As the moment of insertion approaches, the special-operations team climbs aboard. In a hover, the helicopter then lowers its loading ramp into the water, and the chopper crew pushes the loaded craft on its way. Whipped by spray and hot jet wash, the men in the boat fire up the outboard motor and set out. At a prearranged time, the helicopter will return to a designated pickup spot to extricate the team and carry them back to safety.

A boat swallowed whole. A Chinook plucks an inflatable and its five passengers from the surface of a lake during an exercise. The helicopter, loading ramp lowered, descends *(far left)* and comes to a hover upwind of the vessel with the ramp submerged. The aircrew tosses the free end of a winch cable to the men in the inflatable, who clip the line to the bow *(above)*. Hauled up the ramp and into the belly of the chopper *(inset)*, team members grab the nearest handholds in preparation for takeoff. The Chinook then rises—tail high to gain forward speed—as water taken on during the extraction cascades from the rear and through drain holes in the fuselage *(right)*.

A Last Resort

The riskiest of extraction techniques, used only in desperate circumstances, is the Fulton STAR (Surface to Air Recovery) system, also known as Skyhook. Devised by inventor Robert Edison Fulton, Jr., Skyhook is a way of snatching a man on the ground to safety with a modified Air Force MC-130 Combat Talon aircraft flying overhead. Because of the hazards, rehearsals nowadays are restricted to lifting inanimate objects.

The Skyhook procedure begins when the MC-130 paradrops a package containing, among other things, custom clothing, a 500-foot length of special nylon rope, a balloon twenty-three feet long, and helium tanks to fill it. When all is ready on the ground, the aircraft returns for the pickup *(opposite and following pages)*.

Inflating the balloon. A man awaiting extraction by Skyhook begins filling the balloon with helium. The mushroom-shaped bladder will take on the shape of a small dirigible *(far right)* when it has fully expanded.

Awaiting pickup. In a 1960s practice lift, a man clad in a helmet and a nylon coverall with a sewn-in harness awaits pickup. As a safety measure, he also wears a parachute. The risers of his harness are fastened to a nylon lift line, which a helium-filled balloon has raised to a height of 500 feet. For night rescues, a string of flashing lights is tied the length of the rope.

A perfect strike. Flying at about 120 knots, an MC-130 meets the lift line just below the balloon that holds it aloft. The V-shaped apparatus fixed to the nose of the aircraft guides the line toward a clamp in the center. In the event of a miss, cables stretching forward from each wing tip deflect the balloon tether away from the propellers and wings.

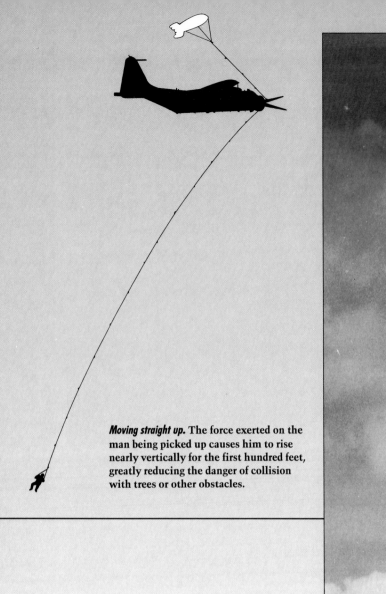

Moving straight up. The force exerted on the man being picked up causes him to rise nearly vertically for the first hundred feet, greatly reducing the danger of collision with trees or other obstacles.

Lifting off. In a picture taken a second or two into an ascent, a man hurtles skyward. Stretch in the nylon lift line makes acceleration smooth and gentle at this point, but when the stretch is exhausted, a powerful jolt occurs. Some who have experienced it say that they feel the harness suit will be ripped away.

Losing the balloon. Connected to the lift line by breakaway cords, the balloon is snapped free by the stress. As the MC-130 speeds up, the lift line approaches the underside of the fuselage.

Winching in the prize. At a speed of 120 knots, the lift line trails close to the belly of the aircraft. From the rear of the plane, crew members lower a hook by rope to catch the nylon tether. They then pull the line into the plane and attach it to a winch that reels it in.

A successful recovery. Four minutes after the clamp at the nose of the aircraft seized the line, the man nears the recovery plane. A crew member stands tethered to the craft, ready to grab him as soon as he is inside.

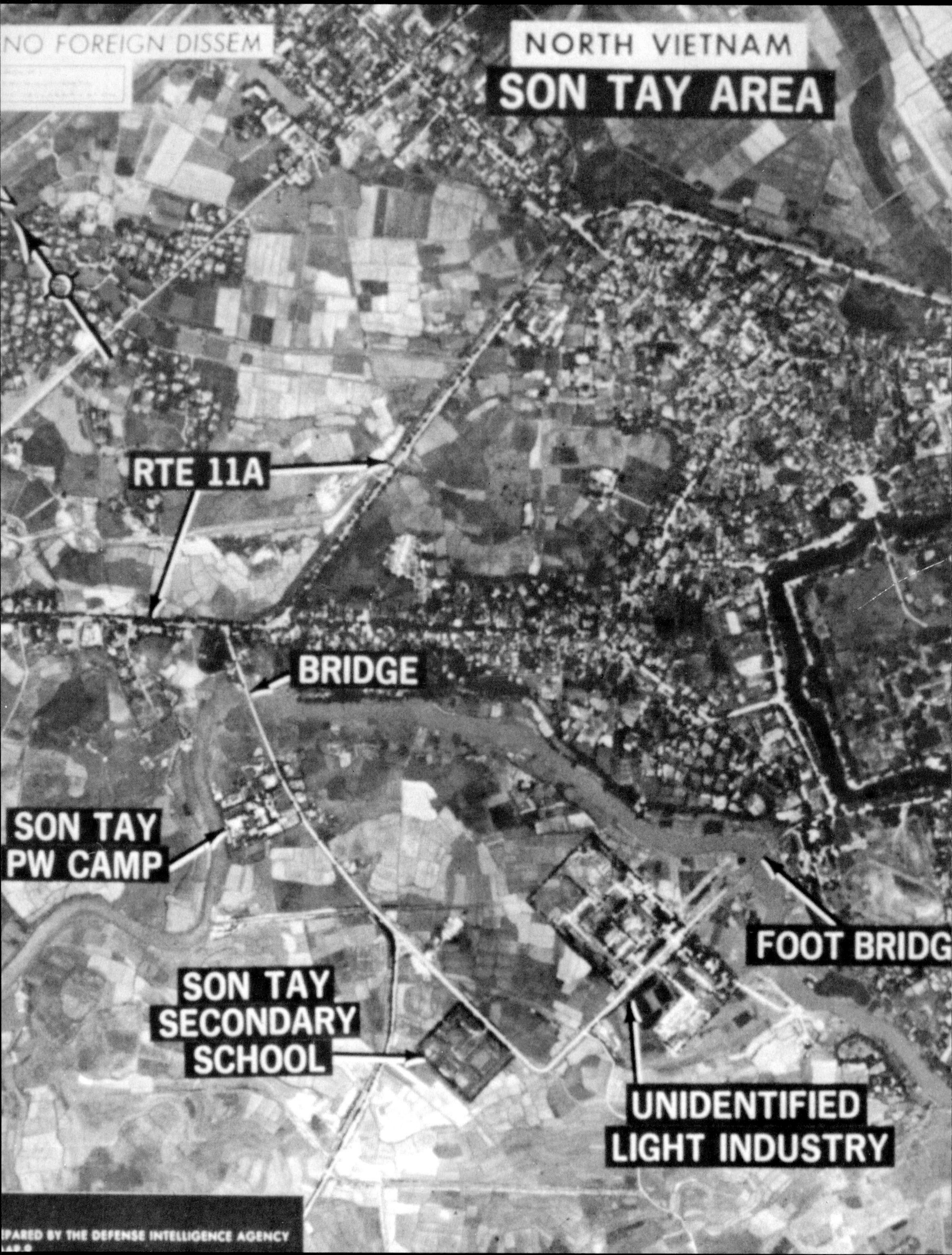

NO FOREIGN DISSEM
NORTH VIETNAM
SON TAY AREA
RTE 11A
BRIDGE
SON TAY
PW CAMP
FOOT BRIDG
SON TAY
SECONDARY
SCHOOL
UNIDENTIFIED
LIGHT INDUSTRY
EPARED BY THE DEFENSE INTELLIGENCE AGENCY

Foray to the Red River Valley

Unusually clear skies on June 6, 1970, allowed a Lockheed SR-71 reconnaissance plane to produce this detailed photograph of North Vietnam's Son Tay prison camp. The square area at right in the picture is the ancient citadel, the center of Son Tay city.

On Thanksgiving eve 1968, fifteen American POWs arrived at a prison camp near the city of Son Tay, twenty-three miles west of downtown Hanoi, North Vietnam. The weather was damp and dismal that day, but the sun appeared the following morning. Taking this as an auspicious sign, the men called their prison Camp Hope.

By the time they reached Son Tay prison, some of the men had been held captive for three years and more in various North Vietnamese prisons, among them the infamous Hoa Lo prison, nicknamed the Hanoi Hilton, and later in another facility called the Zoo. Physical conditions in North Vietnamese camps were abysmal. Cells were cramped, filthy, and vermin-infested. Malaria and dysentery were rampant. Torture and beatings were commonplace.

This prison was an improvement in some ways. In contrast to POWs held at the Hanoi Hilton, those at Son Tay were permitted to spend time outside their cells. The camp was being enlarged, and the prisoners were put to work building a new north wall. They were allowed to wash their clothes and dry them in a shabby courtyard with trees on two sides. Sometimes small groups were taken to chop wood at Mount Ba Vi, a short distance to the southwest.

But torture and inhuman treatment were never far away. For having what their captors termed "bad attitudes," prisoners were clamped in leg irons and obliged to sit on stools for days, without sleep. After climbing up a volleyball pole for a look at the local terrain, Air Force Captain Richard Brenneman was forced to spend thirty days in solitary confinement; his cell was a small wooden shack under one of the guard towers. Although several prisoners at

Son Tay were seriously ill, they were almost always denied medical attention. Air Force pilot Wesley Schierman, for example, developed severe asthma. During the harsh winter of 1969, his desperate gasps for breath could be heard throughout the compound, and his fellow POWs knew that without proper treatment he would die.

The U.S. military's Code of Conduct obliges American prisoners to attempt escape, and the men at Son Tay saw a potential opportunity in their occasional woodcutting excursions. The handful of guards that accompanied them were too numerous simply to run away from, but they could probably be handled by a rescue team, perhaps helicoptered from Laos. But how to attract attention?

The prisoners knew that U.S. reconnaissance aircraft crisscrossed North Vietnam constantly, so they devised ingenious ways to signal. They carefully hung their laundry out to dry in peculiar patterns. POWs working in the courtyard began piling earth, rocks, and coal in odd ways. Guards at Son Tay noticed nothing, but the prisoners counted on sharper observation in Washington. They hoped that, somehow, somebody would decipher the coded messages they were sending. Eventually, somebody did.

Norval Clinebell was an analyst with the Air Force's 1127th Field Activities Group, a collection of intelligence experts stationed at Fort Belvoir, Virginia. Clinebell led a small shop called the Evasion and Escape Branch, which sought information about American POWs for the Central Intelligence Agency (CIA) and the Defense Intelligence Agency (DIA). Sources of data about active POW camps included human observers—NVA soldiers captured in the south who earlier might have seen Americans in a northern prison, high-level defectors, foreign businessmen (known as "friendly travelers") who volunteered their observations, and even American antiwar activists who visited North Vietnam and unintentionally brought back useful intelligence. But Clinebell's group also sifted reams of photographic material that came in from U.S. reconnaissance flights over North Vietnam. Lockheed SR-71 Blackbird aircraft of the Strategic Air Command flew regularly over the countryside at 80,000 feet, taking detailed top-view pictures. Photographs were also provided by Buffalo Hunter drones. Flying at 1,000 feet or so, these pilotless reconnaissance aircraft got a closer look at the ground and supplied informative oblique views of targets.

An old hand at the intelligence game, Clinebell painstakingly pieced together tiny scraps of information even when they were not an obvious fit. In the spring of 1969, his tenacity paid off. By the end of April, Clinebell was convinced that there were two POW camps in the Red River Valley west of Hanoi. One was at Ap Lo, about thirty-one miles from the city. On May 9, he pinpointed the other.

By comparing old and new reconnaissance photographs, Clinebell saw that a walled compound near the city of Son Tay had been recently expanded. A new guard tower had been erected in its northwest corner. In SR-71 photos, he could see men working in the compound. Although the pictures could not reveal their identity, Clinebell observed laundry arranged to form the letters *SAR,* meaning "search and rescue." A pile of rocks seemed to have been laid out in Morse code. The message indicated that six prisoners urgently needed medical attention. Another pile of rocks and earth had been arranged to form the letter *K* (an international symbol meaning "come and get us") with an arrow pointing southwest and the number eight beside it. Clinebell deduced that prisoners were sometimes taken from Son Tay to Mount Ba Vi, eight miles away in the direction of the arrow, in small work parties. The POWs were asking to be rescued from there.

This picture of the camp emerged over more than a year. By May 1970, Clinebell felt that he had assembled incontrovertible evidence of POWs at Son Tay and sent his findings up the military intelligence chain of command. Major General Rockly Triantafellu, the Air Force's Assistant Chief of Staff for Intelligence and a recognized expert in rescue and recovery operations, was convinced that Clinebell was correct. But he wondered why the camp was so distant from the others. All other intelligence indicated that most American POWs were kept in Hoa Lo prison, or very near it. He feared that the prisoners in Son Tay might be the basket cases—men so seriously debilitated by torture that their captors wanted to conceal them from antiwar activists or peace groups.

The Pentagon knew that many POWs were enduring torture. In a 1966 North Vietnamese television appearance, Captain Jeremiah Denton seemed to be blinking oddly. U.S. intelligence experts interpreted the blinking as Morse code for the word *torture.* The Pentagon also learned of torture from North Vietnamese defectors. And by 1970, nine POWs had been released. Most told of humane treatment, but there were also stories of abuse. This made Clinebell's discovery—especially the SAR code—particularly compelling to Pentagon strategists. Musings about a rescue mission began.

It would not be the first time American forces had tried to recover POWs. Between 1966 and 1970, ninety-one rescue operations had been mounted, all inside South Vietnam. Of these, only twenty had succeeded. One difficulty was that POWs were frequently moved from camp to camp. The missions rescued 378 South Vietnamese prisoners, but only one American—Army Specialist, Fourth Class Larry Aiken. However, he was shot by his guards just as the raiding party was about to attack and died fifteen days later.

Evidently, the raid to free Aiken had been compromised at the eleventh hour. If a rescue was to be tried at Son Tay, it would have to be held in utmost secrecy. Triantafellu consulted Brigadier General James R. Allen, the Air Force's Deputy Director for Plans and Policy. Allen summoned two of his top planners for covert operations and gave them a week to come up with a scenario for snatching the Son Tay POWs. He then scheduled a meeting in the Pentagon's inner sanctum with a man he knew would take action.

Army Brigadier General Donald Blackburn was the Pentagon's Special Assistant for Counterinsurgency and Special Activities (SACSA). His career included many forays behind enemy lines, and he was a great believer in the efficacy of small, unorthodox operations. During World War II, he had participated in a hair-raising guerrilla war against the Japanese in the Philippines. In 1960, he had organized covert military advisory groups, known as White Star teams, to operate against Communist units in Laos. These exploits, like his work in the Pentagon, were known only to a select few.

On May 25, 1970, Allen briefed Blackburn on the situation at Son Tay. Afterward the two generals discussed possible plans for a rescue. One idea was to send an agent to Mount Ba Vi from a secret CIA base on the Laotian border. When some prisoners arrived, he could call in a small heliborne force to liberate them. This relatively simple operation would take place with the prisoners out in the clear and isolated from the camp, and with probably only a handful of guards to contend with. But it would also leave most POWs at Son Tay open to reprisals and an uncertain fate.

Allen and Blackburn then discussed a much bolder option. What if a mission was launched to rescue all the prisoners at Son Tay? The

Flanked by North Vietnamese guards, U.S. Air Force pilot Lieutenant Colonel James L. Hughes walks barefoot to Hanoi's International Club for a press conference in 1967. At this point in the Vietnam War, American airmen were being shot down almost daily.

area was remote enough for a lightning raid to be carried out before the NVA could react. Blackburn was enthusiastic and proposed that the raiders should also attempt to rescue the prisoners at Ap Lo. But any raid into North Vietnam would ultimately require approval from the president, Richard Nixon. Putting troops on the ground inside North Vietnam could have political consequences, not only at home but at the on-again-off-again peace talks in Paris.

The route to the top led first through General Earle G. Wheeler, chairman of the Joint Chiefs of Staff (JCS). Realizing that special operations could easily be sandbagged by the Army's conventionally minded staff, Wheeler had said to Blackburn on his appointment as SACSA: "Any time you have problems in this area that you want to discuss, you can come directly to me."

After his conversation with Allen, Blackburn dropped by Wheeler's office. The chairman listened to Blackburn propose striking into the North Vietnamese heartland, then said, "My God, Don, how many battalions is this going to take?" The SACSA assured his boss that, as he saw the operation, it would require only a small group of Special Forces volunteers. Wheeler gave his broad approval, but he wanted a more detailed plan to take before the JCS.

A week later, Blackburn's office had outlined a rescue that would capitalize on the shock of surprise to bring all the prisoners back unharmed: The raid would take place before dawn, when most of the NVA would be asleep; the strike team would be assembled from the cream of the Army's Green Berets; helicopters would transport the raiders and evacuate prisoners; and some kind of air activity over Hanoi or Haiphong would be needed as a diversion. Wheeler was impressed. "I don't know how anyone could say no to this operation," he said. On June 10, the Joint Chiefs gave Blackburn a tentative green light. He gathered a group of experts from the military and civilian intelligence services, installing them in secure offices at Fort Myer, Virginia. They were there to answer one overriding question: Could a rescue succeed?

Just as this team began to examine the issue in earnest, word came from DIA that Ap Lo had been abandoned. Concluding that its prisoners had been moved to another location, Blackburn scrapped the idea for a double rescue and zeroed in on Son Tay.

Focusing on a single camp simplified matters, but as with any military operation, difficulties soon surfaced. Aircraft bearing the strike force would have to penetrate North Vietnamese air space without being detected by radar. Assault teams would be required to land, free the POWs, and leave before the North Vietnamese could react. Moonlight would be needed to see by. North Vietnamese MiGs and SAMs would have to be lured away from the camps. And not a hint of the operation could leak out. Tall as these hurdles might seem, they were deemed surmountable. On July 10, the Joint Chiefs ordered the formation of a Joint Contingency Task Group to begin detailed planning and training.

Blackburn wanted to run the operation himself, but his bosses told him he was needed in Washington to coordinate the planning and execution of the raid with the three branches of the military—no small assignment. While the task force was being trained and equipped at Auxiliary Field 3, a remote site at Eglin Air Force Base, Florida, SACSA would be dealing with Pentagon bureaucrats.

The role so coveted by Blackburn went to forty-nine-year-old Air Force Brigadier General LeRoy Manor. He had flown 72 combat missions as a fighter pilot in World War II, and 275 in Southeast Asia, where he led the 37th Tactical Fighter Wing at Phu Cat, South Vietnam. Presently the commander of the Air Force's Special Operations Force, which trained friendly guerrillas and flew covert missions behind enemy lines, Manor was more than qualified.

Colonel Arthur D. "Bull" Simons, between assignments at Fort Bragg, got the nod as Manor's deputy. He would be the highest-ranking man on the ground at Son Tay. An Army veteran of nearly thirty years, Simons was a legend in Special Forces circles. He had served under Blackburn in Laos and gained renown when, as a White Star team leader, he recruited and trained twelve battalions of Meo tribesmen in a Laotian volunteer army. They were largely responsible for a decrease in North Vietnamese incursions across the Laotian border in the mid-1960s.

A thick neck and broad shoulders earned the cigar-chomping Simons his nickname. Simons was a methodical planner who had brought his 107-man team out of Laos without a single casualty. He was also a fearless, tough-as-nails soldier who believed that bold attacks by small, highly trained groups could inflict great damage on enemy targets and morale. "The more improbable something is," he once said, "the surer you can pull it off." Breaking into an enemy prison camp and rescuing POWs was right up his alley.

Blackburn and Manor worried that Simons might be too old and out of condition to be toting a rifle behind enemy lines. He was fifty-two and had suffered a slight stroke two years earlier. But when Blackburn inquired about his health, Simons announced he was his old self—on parachute status, and back to 250 push-ups a day. Blackburn was satisfied. Even after a stroke, Bull Simons was the best man for the job.

As the planning for the rescue proceeded, it gradually became clear that the mission would require fewer than 100 Special Forces troops. They would have to work quickly. The NVA's 12th Infantry Regiment was based two kilometers away in Son Tay city. Task group intelligence officers judged that enemy troops could reach the prison thirty minutes after the shooting started. Tactical specifics of the plan would be worked out later, during rehearsals.

A hunter both on the job and off, Colonel Bull Simons displays a trophy he bagged in Laos during his 1961 tour of duty with Operation White Star.

Air Force HH-53 helicopters—the Super Jolly Green Giants used to snatch downed pilots from the enemy's grasp—would transport the Green Berets from the Royal Thai Air Force Base (RTAFB) at Udorn, Thailand, and return them there. The plan called for enough such helicopters to fly out as many as 200 prisoners. Besides the Jolly Greens, the Air Force would provide piston-engine A-1 Skyraider fighter-bombers to keep the North Vietnamese at bay should they respond to the attack sooner than anticipated. HC-130 tankers would refuel the helicopters en route, and a pair of MC-130 Combat Talons would guide the choppers and A-1s to Son Tay. The Combat Talons were crucial. The only way to enter North Vietnam without being detected on radar was to sneak in by flying low, behind hills and ridges where radar cannot see. Doing this at night, alone, even in moonlight, was too dangerous for either the helicopters or fighter-bombers. The Combat Talons, however, were equipped with novel forward-looking infrared (FLIR) systems that allowed their pilots to see well enough in the dark to fly safely at treetop level. Dim navigation lights on the planes' wing tips and tails would permit the other aircraft to tag along in safety.

The aircraft would have to cross a treacherous area straddling the Laotian border that was guarded by overlapping coverage from two North Vietnamese antiaircraft radar sites. There seemed to be no

A Warrior's Warrior

From the start of his thirty-year career, Army Colonel Arthur D. "Bull" Simons rarely did anything by the book. The goal of this blunt, barrel-chested, all-business officer was to get the job done, whatever it took.

If part of tactics is making the best of less-than-ideal situations, then Simons was a master. During World War II, while commanding a Ranger company in the Philippines, Simons led his men on a night mission to destroy a Japanese radar station in preparation for the invasion of Leyte. He loaded his team of Rangers into tiny native canoes, which promptly sank. After commandeering additional boats, he landed on the wrong island. He portaged the canoes to the other side, then paddled to the correct island, landing at the base of a cliff behind his target. He and fifteen of his men climbed straight up the cliff—"by our fingernails, you know, I mean straight up," said Simons. When he peered over the top at midmorning, Simons saw a young Japanese soldier dropping his trousers at the latrine. "That's too bad," Simons remembered thinking as he shot the man. Only minutes later, the Rangers put the radar station out of commission.

Balancing Simons's determination to complete a mission sucessfully was an acute sense of responsibility for the safety of his men. "I don't want people to get shot for nothing," he said. "The guy who carries the gun wants to know after the thing goes sour, you are going to be there with him when it's time to come out."

With these qualities, Simons endeared himself to his men and gained their enthusiastic loyalty. Said one of the troops recruited for Operation White Star: "I would follow Bull Simons to hell and back for the sheer joy of being with him on the visit."

way to fly through without being noticed. But National Security Agency experts discovered that one of the radars shut down every night at 2:00 a.m. for five minutes of routine maintenance, opening a short gap in coverage. The strike force would have to time its arrival to thread that gap. This stratagem, and the tactic of terrain hugging, would allow the raiders to approach to within ten minutes of their destination before they could possibly appear on enemy radar screens.

As the helicopters refueled over Laos, squadrons launched from the aircraft carriers *Ranger*, *Oriskany*, and *Hancock* in the Gulf of Tonkin would stage a diversion—a mock attack on Haiphong—to draw the attention of North Vietnam's air defenses away from Son Tay. Because a halt in the bombing of North Vietnam was in effect, the feint would have to rely on parachute flares and the noise from the aircraft.

Weather governed the launch date for the operation. Meteorologists in the planning group recommended waiting until fall, when there would be a hiatus between the thick clouds and heavy rain of the Vietnamese summer and winter monsoons. A rising quarter-moon, between fifteen and forty-five degrees above the east horizon, would be perfect for the rescue party. With this in mind, the weathermen identified two windows of opportunity: a five-day period beginning October 21, and another one beginning a month later.

As the plan jelled, the rescue team was assembled. Simons asked for Lieutenant Colonel Elliott "Bud" Sydnor to be placed in charge of the raiders. Sydnor had a reputation for being fearless in combat, unflustered under pressure, and a dedicated team player—all qualities that would be needed at Son Tay. To lead the team that would actually enter the prison and rescue the prisoners, Simons tapped Captain Richard Meadows. As a sergeant, Dick Meadows once captured several North Vietnamese artillery pieces in Laos at a time when Hanoi was claiming that, contrary to U.S. assertions, the NVA was operating only and entirely within North Vietnam. For his leadership, Meadows was awarded a battlefield commis-

63

sion—to the rank of captain. Simons knew both men well. The three of them had once led a Special Forces team into Laos, where they recaptured a CIA post that had been seized by the NVA. Lieutenant Colonel Joseph Cataldo, a physician with the Special Forces, completed the roster of senior officers. Simons knew that some of the prisoners would be in poor condition and would need a doctor.

On September 8, the proposal was set before the JCS, now presided over by Wheeler's successor, Admiral Thomas Moorer. After cross-examining Blackburn on some of the plan's details, Moorer gave the go-ahead to begin training for the rescue. For the time being, the Washington show-and-tell was over.

Simons began selecting personnel. He, Sydnor, Cataldo, and two Special Forces sergeants major constituted a panel that interviewed 500 volunteers stationed at Fort Bragg, North Carolina. The screenings were sprinkled with questions designed to mislead the candidates as to the nature of the mission, which Simons described as "moderately dangerous." The volunteers were asked if they could scuba-dive, endure long exposure to desert conditions, and whether they suffered from seasickness. After three days, the panel picked 103 Green Berets: 15 officers and 88 enlisted men. All but three had experience in Vietnam. Only half would participate in the mission; the others were trained just in case they were needed.

Meanwhile, blueprints for the raid were becoming more detailed. Reconnaissance photos showed that the prison complex lay in a roughly triangular area bounded by a canal on the south (the base of the triangle), the Song Con River on the west, and a road through the eastern end of the camp. To the north, the road bridged the river; to the south, it curved eastward toward Son Tay city and the 12th NVA Infantry Regiment. Between the camp's southern boundary and the canal lay an open space about a hundred yards square, cultivated in rice paddies that would be dry enough in October and November to serve as a landing zone (LZ) for the helicopters.

The compound where the prisoners were kept was approximately 140 feet wide and 185 feet long. It was enclosed by a wall eight to ten feet high and covered with barbed wire. Guard towers, presumably equipped with machine guns, rose from the northwest and southwest corners, and from the east wall just north of the main gate. Beneath this third tower stood the punishment shack.

The wall enclosed five concrete buildings where, according to photoanalysts, the POWs were incarcerated. Trees edged the small courtyard in the center of the compound from which the POWs had signaled the outside world. Adjacent to the east wall—and extending a few hundred yards north and south—stood several structures tentatively identified as office buildings, a power station, and quarters for guards and their families.

The Green Berets identified four tactical goals: to break quickly into the prison compound, to kill the guards, to block NVA reinforcements, and to move all the prisoners from their cells to waiting helicopters. Simons and his planners, Sydnor and Meadows, decided that three teams would be needed. One would rescue the prisoners; the others would see that nothing interrupted this work.

The rescue team was given the code name Blueboy. Led by Dick Meadows, its fourteen members expected to be flown by helicopter over the prison wall and into the courtyard. Once inside, they would free the prisoners and guide them to safety through a hole they would blow in the wall. All of Blueboy would be carrying CAR-15 automatic assault rifles—a shortened model of the M-16 that would give the men greater freedom of movement as they released prisoners. For extra firepower, the fourteenth man would carry a 7.62-mm M-60 belt-fed machine gun. In addition to a seven-and-a-half-pound explosive charge for breaching the wall, the team would also carry ladders to scale it in case they could not land in the courtyard as planned. Strong bolt cutters were included to bite through the shackles of locks on cell doors and leg irons.

Supporting Blueboy would be teams named Greenleaf and Redwine. Bull Simons would ride with Greenleaf, a twenty-one-man contingent under Captain Udo Walther. These men were responsible for securing the areas generally east of the prison, including the housing quarters for guards and their families. Others were to sprint northward along the road to secure the bridge across the Song Con River for a follow-on demolition team. Greenleaf would carry CAR-15s, an M-60, and two M-79 grenade launchers. Demolition charges would be on hand to blow the hole in the wall, should Blueboy be prevented from accomplishing the task.

Redwine, a nineteen-man team under Captain Dan Turner, was to secure the helicopter landing zone and establish a command post nearby for Bud Sydnor, who would fly in with these men. These responsibilities entailed an assault on a large building thought to be a barracks for guards. The team would blow up a utility pole carrying electricity to the camp and some telephone poles that might interfere with the takeoff of heavily loaded helicopters. Redwine also had to block the road where it intersected the canal south of the camp. To help in this task, the team was equipped with light-amplifying megascopes and carried four M-72 Light Antitank Weapons (LAWs) to stop any NVA armor that might react sooner than expected. When Blueboy began bringing the POWs through the wall, Redwine would help them aboard the helicopters.

Each team would travel to Son Tay as a unit in its own helicopter. As the three teams rehearsed, they experimented to see whether they could compensate for the loss of one or more of the choppers. They found that if only one team made it to Son Tay, the raid could not succeed and would have to be called off. If two teams arrived, they could compensate for their missing comrades well enough to stand a good chance of rescuing the prisoners. Under alternate plan Blue—to be invoked if Blueboy failed to show up—Redwine would assume that team's responsibilities. Similarly, according to plan Red, Greenleaf would fill in for a missing Redwine, and under plan Green, Redwine would carry out Greenleaf's assignments. With these contingencies in mind, each team added to the equipment for its primary missions enough gear to perform its backup tasks.

The plan called for six helicopters. One would use machine guns to attack the corner guard towers. The tower near the gate would be left alone to avoid injuring anyone in the punishment shack. Two more helicopters would deposit teams Greenleaf and Redwine outside the south wall of the camp. The fourth would land Blueboy inside the courtyard. Helicopters five and six, serving as backups, were to set down on an island in Finger Lake several miles away.

As the Green Berets started their preparations, Manor began assembling some of the Air Force's finest helicopter pilots. Major Frederic Donohue, who had logged almost 6,000 hours as a chopper pilot and flown 131 missions in Southeast Asia, would fly the helicopter assigned to knock down the guard towers. Major Herbert Kalen, broadly experienced in rescue operations, would ferry Blueboy. Lieutenant Colonel Warner Britton, Greenleaf's pilot, ran operations and training for the Aerospace Rescue and Recovery Training Center at Eglin. Redwine was paired with Lieutenant Colonel John Allison, a pilot at Eglin. Major Kenneth Murphy and Lieutenant Colonel Royal Brown would fly the backup copters.

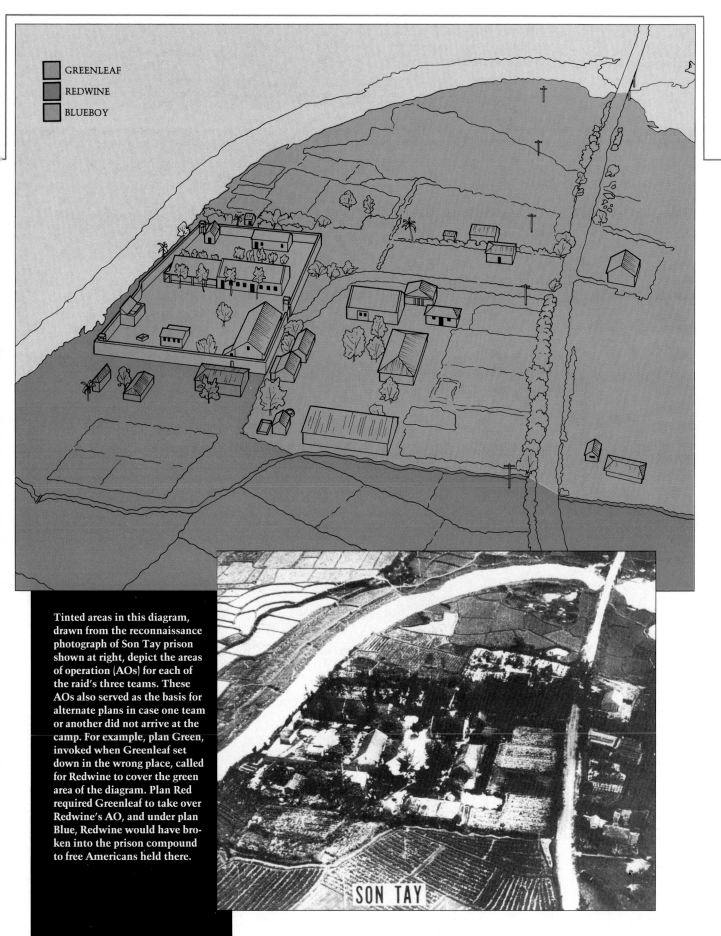

GREENLEAF

REDWINE

BLUEBOY

Tinted areas in this diagram, drawn from the reconnaissance photograph of Son Tay prison shown at right, depict the areas of operation (AOs) for each of the raid's three teams. These AOs also served as the basis for alternate plans in case one team or another did not arrive at the camp. For example, plan Green, invoked when Greenleaf set down in the wrong place, called for Redwine to cover the green area of the diagram. Plan Red required Greenleaf to take over Redwine's AO, and under plan Blue, Redwine would have broken into the prison compound to free Americans held there.

SON TAY

A Model Named Barbara

A meticulously detailed, four-and-a-half-foot-square model—known as Barbara—reproduces all the known features of the Son Tay prison camp, some of which are highlighted below. From left to right, the magnified sections of the model focus on an isolation cell close by an important target—the guard tower at the northwest corner of the camp; the clothesline on which the prisoners hung their wash in such a way as to form coded messages photographed by reconnaissance cameras; and, leaning against a wall, a bicycle that the model builders used to estimate scale for their creation.

Six choppers were needed. Five of them were to be HH-53 Super Jolly Greens. The sixth, Blueboy's helicopter, was to have been a single-engine UH-1 Huey. This craft, however, was only marginally satisfactory—neither as reliable nor as resistant to battle damage as the Jolly Greens, which have two engines. Furthermore, the Huey could not be refueled in flight, forcing a stop in Laos.

The planners solved both problems by choosing an HH-3, the HH-53's predecessor, to carry Blueboy. To set the helicopter down quickly within the narrow confines of the Son Tay courtyard, however, would result in a hard landing as rotor blades cracked against the trees in the courtyard. Dick Meadows and his team felt they could brace themselves well enough to avoid injury on impact, but the craft would be unflyable. It would have to be destroyed where it sat.

As training progressed at Auxiliary Field 3, a life-size mock-up of the prison was built. It was constructed to resemble a large tabletop model of the camp that the CIA had assembled according to measurements taken from reconnaissance photographs. So detailed that it included every tree, the model was nicknamed Barbara and cost $60,000. From the air, said Sydnor, "the mock-up looked like a poor attempt at the Chicago stockyards." Finished by the middle of September, the structure was made of two-by-fours and fabric panels that could be dismantled quickly. The purpose was to hide U.S. preparations from a Soviet surveillance satellite, Cosmos 355, that passed over Eglin twice a day. Daytime practice at the mock-up was limited to the four-hour periods when the satellite was out of range. To prevent the Russians from deducing the rescue attempt and informing their North Vietnamese clients, before each satellite pass during daylight, portions of it were taken down. Manor was so concerned about security that he had the task force's telephones tapped by a team who tried to figure out what was going on by eavesdropping on conversations. Whenever they seemed to be getting warm, Manor would reemphasize to his charges the need for utter circumspection.

No effort was spared to increase the raid's chances. For example, the regular sights on the assault rifles—a post on the barrel that the shooter cen-

Seated in the cabin of a C-130, Dick Meadows *(far left)* and his fourteen-man Blueboy team prepare for the coming raid during a training exercise in September 1970. In the aisle behind three fire extinguishers is a firefight simulator. Much like the device to be dropped from a C-130 at the beginning of the attack, this one was intended to cover the raiders' withdrawal by fooling enemy troops into thinking that the battle was still raging.

ters in a notch in the gun's handle—were useless in the dark, even with a quarter-moon. At Eglin, Simons's best marksmen could hit torso-size targets at fifty meters only 25 percent of the time. Better sights would be required.

In June, Meadows had attended a small-arms conference in California, where he noticed a new kind of night sight. Agreeing that this might be just what was needed, Simons instructed Meadows to order two of the $49.50 devices from the manufacturer—Armalite Corporation of Costa Mesa, California—and mount them on assault rifles for testing. To use the sight, a rifleman kept both eyes open. Looking through the sight with one eye, he saw an illuminated red dot on a black field; with the other eye he looked at his target. The brain combined the two images, and the result was a wide-field vision with a clearly superimposed aiming point. Simons and his

men were thrilled with the result. Using the Armalite single-point sight, the poorest marksman could consistently put all his rounds in a torso-size target at seventy-five meters. The only trouble was that the mountings tended to work loose. This was solved with the generous use of electricians' tape. Sights were ordered for each rifle.

Some of the HH-53 helicopters were to carry a pair of 7.62-mm Miniguns, one mounted in each of the side doors. These six-barrel machine guns, capable of dispensing 4,000 rounds per minute, were used to suppress enemy fire during missions to retrieve downed pilots, always undertaken in daylight. At night, however, the muzzle flash from these weapons blinded the gunners. To solve the problem, conical flash suppressors were custom-made from sheet steel and welded to the ends of the barrels.

Training ran from noon to midnight and later. Many afternoons, the teams rehearsed the raid in concert with the helicopters, firing blanks. For safety during later live-fire practice, the teams performed individually. Following a postmortem and dinner, another rehearsal took place after dark. Just as rigorously, the men drilled themselves in contingency plans Blue, Red, and Green.

For the Blueboy team, removing prisoners from the cells was a top priority. They practiced first by themselves, and then carrying others. Dr. Cataldo, worried that some of the POWs might be so confused that they would struggle after being freed, urged that in the drills, some of the "prisoners" resist being carried. He also had nylon liners sewn into ponchos to keep the prisoners warm and dry during the return flight from Son Tay to Thailand.

As training peaked, ground and air forces held full-scale, seven-hour joint rehearsals, in which the force took off from Field 3, flew a circuitous route through the mountains of Georgia to simulate the flight from Thailand to Son Tay, then landed again at Field 3 to assault the mock-up. This exercise permitted the helicopters to rendezvous with the C-130s, then fly formation with them at radar-evading low altitude—just as they would en route to Son Tay. They practiced aerial refueling, a particularly demanding feat because the top speed of the loaded helicopters—105 knots—was little more than the absolute minimum speed of the laden C-130 tankers.

By early October, timing had become so polished that the aircraft could cross the so-called initial point (IP)—a point on the ground that marks the beginning of the run toward a target—within ninety seconds of the appointed time. Such precision would allow the raiders to slip through the early-morning window in enemy radar coverage, placing them at the walls of Son Tay precisely at 2:18 a.m. Nighttime rehearsals also revealed the benefits to Blueboy and Redwine of prototype light-amplifying contributed by the Army's Night Vision Laboratory at Fort Belvoir, Virginia.

Throughout September, General Manor had conducted briefings on the mission. One was presented to the Joint Chiefs, another to Secretary of Defense Melvin Laird, and a third to the admiral in charge of Pacific operations, including the war in Vietnam. On October 8, Manor, Simons, and Blackburn visited the White House to brief National Security Adviser Henry Kissinger and his assistant, Alexander Haig. Kissinger had an important question. What if the raid failed? he wondered. Wouldn't that mean more Americans—the raiders themselves—being thrown into North Vietnamese prisons? They acknowledged the possibility but nonetheless gave Kissinger "a 95 to 97 percent assurance of success." Manor added that the air crews had logged more than 1,000 flight hours and 268 sorties training for this mission. Kissinger expressed amazement at the thoroughness of the preparations.

Manor said that the task force could be in Thailand and ready for the assault during the first "window of opportunity," which opened October 20. However, they would need approval by the next evening. At this, Kissinger hesitated. He explained that the president, who had been kept abreast of plans for the raid and supported it, would have to give final approval, and he was out of town. Kissinger then voiced misgivings about the timing. On October 24, Nixon would be delivering a speech at the United Nations, and thirty-one heads of state would be dining at the White House. Moreover, congressional elections were coming up in November. A raid on North Vietnam during delicate peace talks could cause trouble at home and abroad. The rescue attempt would have to be postponed.

During the briefing, Blackburn had kept to himself a nagging concern over an apparent decrease in activity at Son Tay. He was almost completely dependent on photographic reconnaissance for information about the camp. But clouds often blocked the high-altitude photography provided by the SR-71s, and the Buffalo Hunter drones were of little help. They could get under the clouds, but at a speed of only 300 knots, they were easy pickings for antiaircraft fire. And even if they were not shot down, their photography often was useless. On one occasion, a Buffalo Hunter drone banked an instant too soon and produced perfect photos of the horizon above Son Tay prison, but no details of the camp itself.

Earlier, there had been no doubt that the camp was active. Overhead photographs showed movement of trucks and cars, and evidence of construction in progress. But between June and early October, the few pictures available revealed a marked decline in these activities. Weeds were growing in the compound. Blackburn concluded that the prisoners were being kept in their cells, but he knew that it could also mean the camp was empty—a dry hole.

SACSA had shared his concern with Admiral Moorer. Nevertheless, on October 27, the chairman approved deployment of the forces to Thailand in time for the second five-day weather window beginning on November 21. His decision, which anticipated presidential approval, seemed to be justified when SR-71 photography of November 2 and 13 showed definite signs of renewed activity at Son Tay in the form of paths trampled in the grass near the guard barracks and shadows from laundry on a clothesline. Photo interpreters called attention once again to a facility—they called it a secondary school—about 450 yards south of the prison. Although the school lay some distance from the Song Con River, the chopper pilots could mistake it for their objective in the moonlight.

By November 14, the C-130s had already arrived at Takhli, Thailand. The ground force showed up a week later. Concurrently, helicopters drawn from squadrons assigned to Southeast Asia moved to Udorn to be readied for the mission. Operation Kingpin, as the rescue mission was now called, was leaning forward.

On the morning of November 18, Moorer presented a final briefing to the president and his advisers in the Oval Office. The POW issue weighed heavily on Nixon. By 1970 there were an estimated 356 Americans in North Vietnamese prisons, and the public wanted them home. Nixon faced criticism that his administration was doing little to speed up their return. He needed a way to demonstrate his commitment to freeing them. At the time of this meeting, there was a new urgency. Five days earlier, the North Vietnamese had told Cora Weiss, a peace activist, that six POWs had died.

Nonetheless, the cautious Nixon asked Moorer for his estimate of "the latest you can wait without fouling Manor up." The admiral replied that the next combination of moonlight and weather wouldn't come until March. "If we're going to make this one, I should send an execute message no later than twenty-four hours from now, sooner if possible," he said. "General Manor and Colonel Simons are in Thailand, ready to launch."

"How could anyone not approve this?" Nixon asked rhetorically. "Hell, if this works, we could even have them here for Thanksgiving dinner, right here in the White House." At Takhli later in the day, Manor received the go-ahead in a coded, high-priority message called a red rocket: Amputate Kingpin.

But now the weather threatened. On November 19, Typhoon Patsy was moving west from the Philippines, bringing 100-mph winds and plenty of clouds and rain. Simultaneously, a cold front was heading south from China. The two were predicted to collide over Hanoi on November 21, the primary day for the mission. It seemed as if the mission would have to be canceled. But Manor's forecasters offered a ray of hope: A ridge of relatively cloud-free high pressure might form over Hanoi, between the typhoon and the cold front, on the twentieth.

As Manor deliberated over the weather, Sydnor's men spent forty-five minutes on the firing range at Takhli, zeroing their sights. They checked their demolition charges and other gear. Each reviewed his own escape and evasion plan.

Call signs were issued for the helicopters. The HH-3 carrying Captain Meadows and Blueboy would be Banana 1. Simons, Walther, and Greenleaf would be Apple 1, Sydnor with Turner and his Redwine group would be Apple 2, and Donohue's gunship would be Apple 3. The reserve Jolly Greens would be Apple 4 and Apple 5.

On the twentieth, just as the meteorologists had predicted, the ridge of high pressure appeared. A reconnaissance flight confirmed that the weather was right. Manor agonized, then decided to launch the mission a day early. The ground force had lunch and took sleeping pills issued by Dr. Cataldo. At 3:56 p.m., while they slept, Manor signaled from his command post at Monkey Mountain, a peak bristling with electronic gear a few miles west of Da Nang in South Vietnam. The mission was a go. The men woke at 5:00 p.m., had dinner, and an hour later, assembled for their final briefing.

It was then that Simons answered the question that had crossed each soldier's mind many times in the past four months: Exactly where were they going, and whom were they going to save? By this time, the participants had guessed much about the mission. It had become clear that they were going to free several individuals from

Members of Redwine conduct a final equipment check shortly before departing from Takhli Air Force Base, Thailand, for Udorn. In the foreground are landing lights, attached to beanbags for ease of placement. The weapons shown here are CAR-15 assault rifles, and the headsets are ear protectors worn to absorb the noise of explosions at Son Tay.

captivity. While planning escape and evasion routes back to Laos for use in case something went wrong, the troops deduced that they were headed for North Vietnam. About the only thing they did not know was the name of their objective—and that their current deployment was not just another drill.

"We are going to rescue seventy American prisoners of war, maybe more, from a camp called Son Tay," Simons announced. "This is something American prisoners have a right to expect from their fellow soldiers. The target is twenty-three miles west of Hanoi." The room went silent. A few soldiers let out subdued whistles.

"You are to let nothing interfere with this operation," Simons added. "Our mission is to rescue prisoners, not to take prisoners. If there's been a leak, we'll know it as soon as the second or third chopper sets down; that's when they'll cream us. If that happens, I want to keep this force together. We will back up to the Song Con River, and let them come across that open ground. We'll make them pay for every foot." The men stood up, cheered, and applauded.

The next few hours were consumed with final equipment checks. Every piece of gear had been assigned to a team member, and other members knew exactly who had what. This meant that equipment could be swapped or borrowed if needed. The teams were then given their daunting ammunition load. For the CAR-15s and M-16s, a total of almost 20,000 cartridges were carried. There were more than 1,162 rounds for .45-caliber pistols, 219 grenades for the M-79 launchers, 4,300 rounds for the M-60 machine guns, 100 shotgun shells, 11 demolition charges, and 213 hand grenades. Among the more heavily burdened was Sergeant Gregory McGuire. This 205-pound soldier would step off Apple 2 carrying well over 100 pounds. His task was to set up the roadblock where the road crossed the canal near the camp.

At 10:32 p.m., the raiders took off from Takhli for Udorn, where they boarded the helicopters. There was a scare as the number three engine on one of the Combat Talons balked at starting. Manor radioed word from Monkey Mountain to take off with three engines if necessary. Finally, the recalcitrant engine came to life. At 11:18 p.m., the last chopper lifted off and retracted its landing gear. In just three hours, the men would surge from the helicopters shooting.

Aboard Apple 1, Bull Simons settled in for a nap, leaving orders to be roused twenty minutes away from the objective.

Two hours later, as the strike force refueled over Laos, it was joined by the other C-130 leading the Skyraiders *(map, page 79)*. Far to the east, the Navy launched the diversion. Fifty-eight aircraft catapulted from the carriers in the Gulf of Tonkin: twenty-seven A-7 and ten A-6 attack planes, seven EKA-3B electronic-countermeasures aircraft, two E-2B airborne warning and control aircraft to watch for MiGs, as well as six F-8 and six F-4 fighters to shoot them down.

Guided by the Combat Talons, the strike force descended into North Vietnam through a scattered layer of clouds at 2,000 feet, and leveled off at a terrain-hugging 500 feet. In Apple 1, someone nudged Simons awake. The helicopters reached the IP one minute ahead of schedule. Then checkpoints came up, just as anticipated. First was the Black River, ten miles from Son Tay. Then Finger Lake, seven miles west, followed by a northerly bend in the Song Con River, two miles from the prison. The skies were clear. To the east, the pilots could see the lights of Hanoi. Suddenly, flares dropped by the Navy aviators lit up Haiphong harbor.

Donohue in Apple 3 corrected his course to compensate for a slight northerly cross wind and scrutinized the landscape. Now he was on his own. The first Combat Talon, having led the helicopters almost to within sight of the prison, had climbed to 1,500 feet. After dropping a parachute flare to light the LZ, it would then immediately bend south to drop firefight simulators—firecrackers woven into a pallet-size plastic mat to confuse the NVA by mimicking the pop of small arms fire some distance from the real action—and napalm to serve as a beacon to help the A-1s circle within less than a minute's flight time of the camp. Then the C-130 would head for home. The second C-130 would orbit a few miles away, waiting to lead the helicopters back to Thailand after the raid.

The flare popped at 2:18 a.m. As it lit up Donohue's cockpit, a warning light came on indicating trouble in the transmission that linked the helicopter's six-bladed rotor to the engines. Ordinarily, Donohue would have landed immediately. Now he pressed on.

Looking ahead, the pilot saw the prison compound—or thought he did. But the cross wind had carried Apple 3 a little farther south than its pilot realized, leading him to mistake the nearby "secondary school" for Son Tay. His copilot, Captain Tom Waldron, caught the error just in time, and Donohue veered left toward the correct target, now just seconds away.

Donohue raised the nose of the helicopter, using the rotor wash to slow down, then leveled off just above the treetops and floated slowly across the camp. His door gunners sent deadly 4,000-round-per-minute tracer streams into two guard towers, setting fire to the one at the northwest corner of the camp. Donohue landed at his holding point in a nearby rice paddy.

Next on the scene was Blueboy in Banana 1. As the pilot, Major Kalen, headed for the crash-landing inside the compound, he noticed that some of the trees seemed much taller than the forty feet he had expected. Rotor blades whacked tree limbs. One blade severed a ten-inch tree trunk, causing a lurch to the right at nearly a forty-degree angle. In the cabin, Meadows and his men were shooting at the guard towers from the helicopter's doors and windows. The chopper hit the ground so hard that the jolt tossed one of the Green Berets through the side door. It also dislodged a fire extinguisher that fell on the crew chief, breaking his ankle.

Meadows was shaken, but he sprang from the damaged helicopter and put the bullhorn to his mouth. "We're Americans," he shouted. "Keep your heads down. This is a rescue. We're here to get you out. Get on the floor. We'll be in your cells in a minute."

Blueboy's men wasted no time. They sprayed the guard towers with fire from their CAR-15s to make sure the sentinels in them were dead. Blueboy's demolitionist, Master Sergeant Billie Moore, ran to the outer wall of the compound to blow open an exit path. "I tried to place my special charge using three different types of tape," he would write the next day. "Nothing would stick. I then tried a nail. The cement would not hold, so I placed the spare charge of three blocks of C-4 at the foot of the wall and ignited the charge. It blew a hole about four by four feet." Two teams of four men began to open cell doors, only one of which was locked. As the flares overhead sputtered out, a small group of NVA trapped inside the

Gesturing with his trademark cigar, Bull Simons delivers an inspirational pep talk at Takhli just minutes before his raiders were to embark on the mission. In addition to a holstered pistol under his arm, Simons carries an eighteen-inch machete in a tooled leather sheath.

77

compound tried to escape through the gate in the east wall. Armed, but only partly dressed and obviously confused, they made easy targets in the firelight. Just two minutes and thirty seconds had passed since Banana 1 came to rest in the prison courtyard.

As Blueboy was seizing control of the compound, Lieutenant Colonel Allison steered Apple 2, carrying Sydnor and the Redwine team, toward his landing point outside the prison's south wall. Immediately he knew something had gone wrong. The helicopter with Walther's Greenleaf team and Simons aboard—supposed to be landing just to the east—was nowhere in sight. Redwine would now have to do their own job of blocking the south road and securing the LZ, plus that of Greenleaf.

Approaching to land, Allison ordered his door gunners to open up on the guard buildings that had been Greenleaf's responsibility. Once again Minigun fire darted over the camp. Tracer rounds ignited the building. One guard staggered out with a rifle and began to fire at Apple 2. A Minigun blast knocked him over, but amazingly he kept shooting. Seconds later, another blast from the Minigun killed him. Apple 2 touched down, and Redwine poured down the ramp at the rear of the helicopter. Sydnor radioed that plan Green was in effect, and Allison flew the helicopter to its holding position in a nearby rice paddy.

One Redwine soldier destroyed a nearby utility pole with a demolition charge. A small group raced down the camp road to the south, killed two NVA soldiers, and set up a roadblock about a hundred yards from the LZ. By chance, trucks were traveling on the road south of the prison; the roadblock team blew them up with LAWs. Pathfinders—Green Berets specially trained in helicopter operations—marked the LZ with flashing lights to make it easy for the helicopter pilots to land when they returned to pick up the raiding party and their prizes.

A four-man assault team headed toward the prison. Their job was to clear a large barracks outside the southeast corner of the compound. One of the team, Sergeant Herman Spencer, was delayed breaking through bushes laced with wire that the NVA had threaded through them. As a result, the man to his right, Sergeant Joseph Murray, was alone and exposed when he reached the barracks.

Murray could see guards inside "scurrying like mice," trying to grab weapons and join the fight. To prevent his own injury by shrapnel, Murray had planned to toss a concussion grenade into the

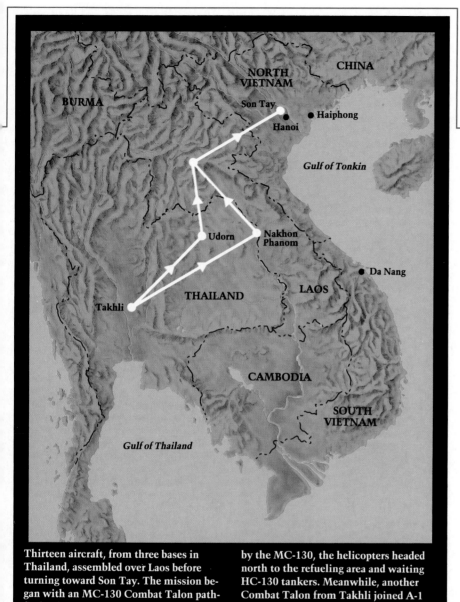

building, then use his rifle on the stunned guards. But with Spencer unable to protect him on the left—and with Greenleaf's protection missing from the right—Murray instead pulled a fragmentation grenade from his belt. As he yanked out the pin and threw the grenade, he heard firing to his rear. Certain that his number was up, Murray turned to face his antagonists—three NVA soldiers.

Spencer, meanwhile, had disentangled himself from the hedge and run to Murray's aid. He dropped two of the guards within twenty feet of his beleaguered comrade. The third was six feet from Murray when Spencer shot him dead. Murray had taken a round in the thigh. But it broke no bone, and he could still fight. So they moved on.

Nearby, some guards running to escape actually bumped into the Americans, recoiling in horror before being shot. Three NVA troops trying to dash to safety from the

Thirteen aircraft, from three bases in Thailand, assembled over Laos before turning toward Son Tay. The mission began with an MC-130 Combat Talon pathfinder departing Takhli for Udorn, where the raiders had boarded helicopters. Led by the MC-130, the helicopters headed north to the refueling area and waiting HC-130 tankers. Meanwhile, another Combat Talon from Takhli joined A-1 Skyraiders based at Nakhon Phanom and led them to the rendezvous.

barracks were cut down with a single shotgun blast and hit again as they fell. Of the fifty-odd guards at Son Tay, nearly all were killed.

Meanwhile, Simons and Greenleaf were 450 meters south of the camp, waging a spectacular battle of their own at the "secondary school." Apple 1 pilot Lieutenant Colonel Britton had mistaken this complex for the prison camp. Concentrating on landing, he did not notice the other helicopters veer toward the correct target. So he discharged Greenleaf in the wrong place, taking off immediately for his holding position.

Simons and Walther realized the error at once. They couldn't hear Meadows on the bullhorn, a deep trench wasn't where it was sup-

Choreography of an Assault

As shown in the illustration at right, Blue-boy *(blue arrows)* crash-landed inside the compound. One team member advanced to blow a hole in the west wall of the compound, while others dashed to the prison buildings to free the inmates.

Meanwhile, helicopter door gunners of Redwine *(red arrows)* blasted guard buildings with their Miniguns. After landing, Redwine pathfinders set up lights to mark the area for the helicopters' return. Other members of the team established roadblocks, cleared buildings that lay generally south of the wall, and made their way to a hole blown by Blueboy. Redwine also neutralized some of the structures in Greenleaf's area of operations; inserted at the wrong location, Greenleaf was delayed by a brief but intense firefight, tardiness that triggered alternate plan Green.

Arriving at Son Tay several minutes later than the others, Greenleaf *(green arrows)* resumed control of its AO from Redwine. But by then, Blueboy had discovered that Son Tay's cells were empty, and all the troops were recalled to the helicopters. From landing to takeoff, the entire operation lasted only twenty-six minutes.

posed to be, and inside the walls stood a two-story building. Son Tay had only single-story structures.

Overhead, Colonel Jay Straher, copilot in Apple 2, was the first to break radio silence. He informed Britton that he had put Greenleaf down in the wrong place. From the ground came a cryptic recall message from Simons's radio operator. There was no time for more. Automatic weapons fire was coming from the building. This was no secondary school. It was a military post with score upon score of well-armed enemy troops.

ut Greenleaf had the advantage of surprise. The men began returning fire immediately. Enemy soldiers, dressed only in their underwear and carrying no weapons, desperately tried to escape. Udo Walther killed four as they fled. He then walked up to one bay of the building and tossed in a hand grenade. After it went off, he entered the room and hosed it down with his CAR-15. He went from one bay to another doing this while a Green Beret waited outside to cut down the enemy as they tried to flee. It seemed that only some of the foe were Vietnamese. Later it would be judged that the foreigners Greenleaf encountered were Chinese advisers, most likely there to train gunners for antiaircraft artillery.

Simons ducked into a trench to wait for Apple 1's return. He calmly lit a cigar. Unexpectedly, a terrified enemy soldier jumped into the trench—armed, but wearing only his underpants. "He looked at me like I was made of green cheese," Simons said later. "I remember thinking, 'this is no time for introductions.'" Simons emptied his .357 Magnum handgun into the man's chest.

Meanwhile, in Apple 1, Britton saw tracers being fired where he had deposited Greenleaf. By the time he heard the recall from Simons's radio operator, he was already wrenching the helicopter into a turn to head back. He landed again two minutes after taking off, and four minutes into the raid the men reboarded the helicopter.

Thirty seconds later, Greenleaf landed at Son Tay. Sydnor radioed Blueboy and Redwine to revert to the basic plan. Once on the ground, the Greenleaf team carried out their remaining tasks. Redwine finished the job of securing the east end of the prison compound and killing the few guards remaining there.

By this time, there was little resistance left. But Sydnor had bad news from Meadows. "Negative items," he radioed, using the prearranged code word for prisoners. "Count complete."

Sydnor did not dwell on the disappointment. He promptly ordered his troops to withdraw and recalled Apple 1 and Apple 2 to the landing zone to pick them up. Twenty-two minutes after the raid began, twenty-five Green Berets departed in Apple 1. As Apple 2 arrived and the rest of the men were loading, ground commander Sydnor issued the code word "Free Swing," which gave authority to the Skyraiders to engage all targets. At the same time, demolitionist Billie Moore climbed into the wreckage of Banana 1 in the courtyard and pulled the fuze lighter that would detonate charges packed between two of the helicopter's fuel tanks. Moore then hustled back through the hole he had blown in the wall earlier and joined the thirty-three other men aboard Apple 2. Six minutes after the big ship lifted into the darkness, the men saw a huge fireball as Banana 1 exploded.

As the men unwound from the mission at Udorn and prepared to rejoin their units, Colonel Simons and General Manor were summoned to Washington. Arriving a couple of days later, they huddled with their superiors over breakfast on November 23 and decided to announce the raid and its heartbreaking results in a news conference that afternoon. Why, the press wanted to know, had the United States attacked an empty camp?

Aerial photography, valuable as it can be for gathering intelligence, is much better at revealing a presence than an absence. No sign of something may mean only that it is well concealed. Prisoners confined indoors—as they might well have been had the North Vietnamese discovered their attempts to communicate with the outside world—would leave no clue that they were there, even though they had gone nowhere.

A human observer on the scene could have confirmed the presence of prisoners, but putting an untested pair of eyes at Son Tay or inserting a recon team just before the raid invited disclosure. A network of trustworthy agents inside North Vietnam had once existed, but it had been deactivated by President Lyndon Johnson in 1968. Such a system takes years to build, and it could not be replaced in time. However, word had reached the DIA in Washington just three days before the raid that a North Vietnamese government official had smuggled out of the country a list of active POW camps. Son Tay was not on it. But this official was not yet a proven source of anything except the most innocuous information. Intelligence

Shot one day after the raid, a section of an SR-71 photograph shows the scars of battle at Son Tay. *LZs* mark helicopter landing zones; pieces of Blueboy's wrecked chopper are visible in the left central portion of the compound. Damaged roofs, charred guard quarters, and a flattened power pole convey the violence of the action.

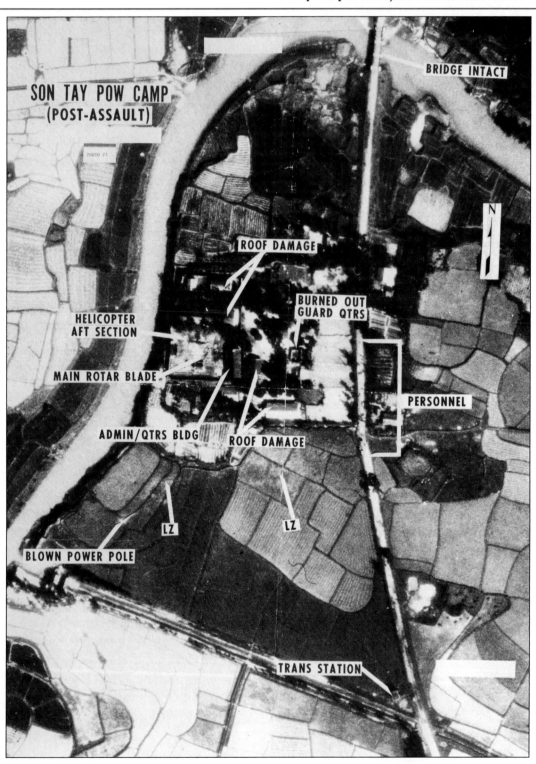

SON TAY POW CAMP
(POST-ASSAULT)

PHOTO 82

BRIDGE INTACT

N

ROOF DAMAGE

BURNED OUT
GUARD QTRS

HELICOPTER
AFT SECTION

PERSONNEL

MAIN ROTAR BLADE

ADMIN/QTRS BLDG   ROOF DAMAGE

LZ

LZ

BLOWN POWER POLE

TRANS STATION

analysts had no corroborating report, and when pressed by Blackburn, they could not say for certain that Son Tay was empty. So Admiral Moorer decided to go ahead with the operation. Better to raid an empty camp than to abandon the effort and discover later that the prisoners were there waiting.

Blackburn likewise had little sympathy with calling off the mission. He had long and fruitlessly advocated strikes by Rangers or Special Forces deep into North Vietnam and hoped to show with this raid that such operations could succeed. "I was looking for any straw I could find to keep the mission alive," he said later. "I wanted to demonstrate that we could get in there and pull their chain."

It eventually emerged that all the POWs at Son Tay had been moved twelve miles east, to Dong Hoi, on July 14. According to Colonel Richard Dutton, an Air Force F-105 pilot held at Son Tay and released in 1973, there was nothing suspicious about the transfer. A prison had been under construction at Dong Hoi for some time. When it was finished, the prisoners were moved.

In the early hours of November 21, Dutton and his fellow POWs at Dong Hoi heard the commotion above Haiphong and from the direction of Son Tay, but for several days they did not know for certain what had happened. By that time, they and all the other American prisoners in North Vietnam had been consolidated at Hoa Lo prison in Hanoi. Because of a shortage of cells there, they bunked together in huge bays. For the first time, they were able to see and talk to each other and to set up a chain of command within their ranks—all tremendous morale boosters. Also held here were a number of Vietnamese political prisoners. Their jailers ranted at them with an account of the raid on Son Tay—news that the Vietnamese passed to the Americans. It gave them a terrific lift to learn that their countrymen had actually tried to come get them.

Perhaps Sergeant Murray best summed up the rescue effort. "When I looked out the side door," he remembered many years later of helicoptering away from the empty prison camp, "SAMs were being punched off indiscriminately, like flaming telephone poles into the night. The 53 was silent. No chatter. For twenty minutes, we had owned a piece of North Vietnam, and to this day we know full well that if the prisoners had been there, they would have been free that night. Nothing could or would have stood in our way to successfully complete that mission except what we encountered—no prisoners at Son Tay." ★★

Spencer, meanwhile, had disentangled himself from the hedge and ran to Murray's aid. He dropped two of the guards within twenty feet of his beleaguered comrade.

A Cudgel in Asia; a Scalpel in Africa

A Soviet convoy rolls toward Kabul in February 1980 to shore up the Communist puppet regime in Afghanistan. Taken through the betasseled windshield of an Afghan intercity bus, this picture was made covertly; discovery could have landed the European photographer in an Afghan jail.

On Christmas Eve of 1979, a column of Soviet armor clanked across the border between the republic of Turkmenistan and Afghanistan, headed for Kabul. The advance marked the end of preparation and the beginning of action in an invasion that had been aplanning since summer. In the preceding weeks, some 5,500 troops—among them hundreds of Spetsnaz special-operations troops disguised as civilians—had arrived in the land of the Khyber Pass. The Spetsnaz mission would be to paralyze the Afghan government and its armed forces through a variety of sharp actions that included capturing the national radio station, taking over the airport in Kabul, and seizing the country's president.

Special operations typically involve use of the smallest force possible. Even so, the size of the element dispatched on a mission can vary greatly according to the objective. Discreet action in politically sensitive circumstances, for example, all but demands a team numbering no more than a handful of men, perhaps as few as two or three. Reconnaissance deep into enemy-held territory argues for a larger team—perhaps as many as twenty—that can defend itself should it be detected.

Where a fight is anticipated, more men are needed. Mounting the raid against the Son Tay prison camp required some fifty U.S. Special Forces troops. To seize an airfield, the Rangers expect to send at least 150 men and perhaps many more, depending on enemy defenses. And in planning the capture of the Afghan head of state,

SOVIET UNION

AFGHANISTAN

the Soviets seem to have anticipated fierce resistance, dispatching a combined force of perhaps 2,000 Spetsnaz and airborne troops. On the sledgehammer-to-scalpel spectrum of special operations, this mission represented an extreme.

At the pinnacle of power in Afghanistan was Hafizullah Amin. Seeing him switch food and drink with others at the dinner table, a stranger might have mistaken the man for one of the Borgias—the conniving fifteenth-century Italian family whose factions poisoned each other with apparent abandon over seemingly trivial matters. President Amin had good reason to be wary. After all, his two predecessors had been murdered, one in a gun battle the year before, and the other some weeks earlier at the hands of Amin's own burly bodyguards, who smothered him with pillows. Indeed, Amin was just as close to breathing his last as he imagined. Unbeknown to him, his personal cook was an agent of the Soviet KGB with the mission of poisoning him.

Amin's successful efforts to avoid a fatal dinner were a frustration to the KGB. The trouble was that Amin's cook got cold feet. He had been provided the latest in poisons, a chemical that left no telltale traces in the body and produced the appearance of a heart attack or a stroke. But the president's well-known distrust of his own victuals would point toward the kitchen if something happened, and in Kabul, the finger of suspicion differed little from a death sentence.

Although the KGB had been charged with disposing of Amin, they were reluctant participants in a chain of events that had begun some six years earlier with the 1973 overthrow of the Afghan king by a leftist named Muhammad Daoud. During his tenure as prime minister a decade earlier, Daoud had helped tie Kabul to Moscow, a move that pleased Soviet political leaders. But his Western education and contacts were cause for some concern in the Kremlin, especially within the Soviet intelligence organ. KGB officials, ever watchful of political loyalty, feared that Daoud might be a change for the worse.

And so he was. By 1977, Daoud had turned to other nations for military assistance and expelled Soviet military advisers from some army units, moves that betrayed a growing independence of the

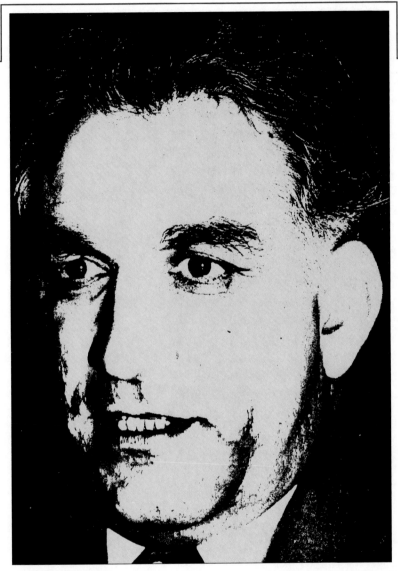

A ruthless intriguer, Communist Hafizullah Amin became Afghanistan's president after arranging the assassination of his predecessor, Noor Muhammad Taraki. Three months later, Amin was killed in turn—by the Russians, who considered him unstable and dangerous. Amin was a graduate of Columbia University Teachers College in New York City.

USSR. In 1978, Daoud turned on Moscow and began arresting Afghan Communists. A Soviet-supported coup resulted in the bloody death of Daoud, who was replaced by Noor Muhammad Taraki, a Communist and the personal choice of Soviet General Secretary Leonid Brezhnev. Taraki soon had his country realigned with Moscow, but all was not well. The KGB knew Taraki as something of a paranoid and, true to his dossier, he began a brutal repression of all opposition, real or imagined. Within a year of assuming power, he alienated Afghan Muslim fundamentalists and their powerful spiritual leaders, the mullahs. As a consequence, Taraki needed an increasing number of Soviet advisers and military supplies to stay in power.

In March 1979, in the Afghan city of Herāt, resentment turned into violence. As people gathered in a chill wind to protest Communist rule, some Afghan soldiers joined in, adding spine to the crowd. Stones were thrown. Soon the protesters broke into a government arsenal and began passing weapons to eager hands. Angry Afghans ran through the streets, searching out and butchering Russian advisers and their families. Five days passed before loyal Afghan troops and Soviet units could reach Herāt. Vengeance was swift and brutal. Estimates of the death toll among the city's inhabitants range as high as 5,000.

Taraki was clearly a liability, but the alternative was even less palatable. This was Amin. So abhorrent was he to the Soviets that they helped Taraki try to murder him—twice. But in having his rival smothered, Amin won out.

As predicted in Moscow, the situation in Afghanistan worsened

under Amin. Muslim leaders, recognizing the new man as just another Communist puppet of the Soviets, called for a jihad—a holy
war against the nonbelievers. Every one of Afghanistan's provinces
took up arms. Already-devout tribesmen became fanatical Mujahedin, soldiers of the jihad who singled out the hated infidels as
targets. Captured Soviet advisers were reportedly flayed alive and
subjected to other atrocities. Within months, the riot in Herāt had
exploded into a conflict that at least one Russian general would
later call the Soviet Union's Vietnam.

The KGB thought the situation might be salvageable. They believed the growing Soviet presence throughout the country would
be sufficient to keep Amin under control without ousting him. But
Brezhnev overrode his intelligence advisers and ordered another
change of government in Kabul—this time to coincide with a full
invasion aimed ostensibly at the Mujahedin. Small-scale deploy-
ments into the country began in September. Soon thereafter, U.S.
intelligence began reporting large troop movements in the Soviet
republic of Turkmenistan and other regions bordering Afghanistan.

Amin may have suspected the coming deployment of Soviet
troops, but he almost certainly had not asked for it. Knowing of the
Soviet hand in the demise of his predecessors and in attempts on his
own life, he must have felt uneasy at the mere thought of Russian
intervention. And well he might, for there was a sinister and secret
phase of the invasion. While the bulk of the Soviet military machine fanned out against the guerrillas, a force of Spetsnaz commandos would take aim at the president himself.

Spetsnaz. The name itself resonates like the metallic snick from the
bolt of an AK-47. To the Mujahedin, they would become known and
feared as "the black soldiers" because of the dark makeup they
apply to their faces for night operations. Only men of the highest
caliber are chosen for Spetsnaz—each graded for mental and physical prowess and loyalty to the regime. The soldiers are two-year
conscripts drafted mainly from rural areas and poorly informed
about the West. The officers are the cream of the professional cadre.
Spetsnaz is given priority in recruitment over other elite forces such
as the airborne, rocketry, and submarine forces.

All are trained in hand-to-hand fighting, silent killing techniques,
parachuting, sabotage, infiltration, lock picking, and foreign lan-

guages. Their existence is cloaked in secrecy, and recruits sign an oath acknowledging death as the punishment for divulging details about their service. Often they are detached from their units, posing as boxers, wrestlers, martial-arts experts, and marksmen. According to one defector, they sometimes show up on Olympic teams.

Spetsnaz commandos are trained to operate hundreds of kilometers behind enemy lines, spearheading the advance of Soviet armies by sowing confusion through sabotage and assassination. The basic operational unit is a team of up to fifteen men. Western intelligence analysts report that during the early 1970s, four-man Spetsnaz squads secretly entered Vietnam to test the new Dragunov SVD sniper rifle under combat conditions. In 1982, naval Spetsnaz frogmen would pilot minisubmarines far into Swedish waters and take up temporary positions just off Stockholm.

As a prelude to the invasion of Afghanistan, Soviet Army General Aleksey Yepishev, head of the armed forces Political Administration, toured the country in April 1979. He was followed to Afghanistan in August by General Ivan Grigoriyevich Pavlovskiy, commander of all Soviet ground forces, who stayed two

Taking the sun, Soviet advisers survey the city of Kabul, Afghanistan, from their hotel balcony in September 1979, just a few months before Russian troops invaded the country. In all, there were at least 8,000 Soviet soldiers and civilian consultants in Afghanistan before the invasion. Their presence stirred great popular resentment. "I don't just want all the Soviets to leave," said one businessman. "I want to see them all die."

Training Leaders for Spetsnaz

Officer candidates in the elite Ryazan Airborne School practice hand-to-hand combat as part of their tough physical training. These soldiers are partway through a rigorous selection process that may lead a few of them into the *voiska spetsialnogo naznacheniya*—the Soviet special-operations force commonly known as Spetsnaz.

The screening begins for some of the men when they are only ten years old. At that age, they are already being watched for the first signs of the physical fitness and political reliability that may qualify them some years later for membership in the Young Communist League. From these youths come candidates for airborne-officers training. And some of these graduates will eventually serve in Spetsnaz.

The weeding-out process is rigorous. Although there is universal military service in the Soviet Union, only a handful of men are picked for airborne-officers training—about 500 a year out of more than 30,000 applicants. The officer candidates graduate from a four-year course with the equivalent of a university degree in military engineering. Their progress is periodically reviewed by a special committee from the GRU (Soviet military intelligence), and the cream of the group are selected for Spetsnaz. They then undergo further training in special schools, and upon completion of the course, they are entitled to pick their own men for training as enlisted Spetsnaz personnel.

Like most other special-operations forces, Spetsnaz troops are required to be skilled in an astonishing variety of functions—including parachuting, radio operation, intelligence gathering, assassination techniques, neutralization of nuclear weapons, and the disruption of air-defense, communications, and economic systems.

months, during which detailed plans were laid for the December invasion. In September, as the first troop movements associated specifically with the invasion took place, the Soviets landed three battalions of paratroops—nearly 900 men—at Bagram air base, forty miles from Kabul. The purpose was to ensure possession of the airfield to receive transports that would pour troops into Afghanistan during the initial stages of the invasion.

On December 8 and 9—just a couple of weeks before the balloon was to go up on Christmas Eve—another 2,500 Soviet troops, some of them equipped with tanks and artillery, flew into the Bagram air base to join the force that was already there. The Soviets also supplemented their forces at other strategically situated airfields and took over security for the Salang Tunnel through the mountains that lay between Kabul and Turkmenistan. In the Soviet Union itself, recently alerted armored units assumed positions near the border town of Termez and the terminus of a Russian-built road that stretched to the Afghan capital.

On December 24, the movement of Soviet forces into Afghanistan began in earnest. The armored divisions crossed the frontier and rumbled toward Kabul. Over a period of two days, a massive airlift of nearly 200 flights delivered 10,000 airborne and Spetsnaz troops to Afghanistan's interior. Simultaneously, Soviet advisers neutralized the two Afghan armored divisions nearest the city by calling in tank batteries for winterization. In another ploy, they ordered the collection and inventory of antitank weapons and recalled a number of vehicles, ostensibly to correct a "defect." The Afghans could not have mounted an effective resistance even if they had wished to.

With the spearhead of the invasion in place, Kabul was about to be taken down. Weeks earlier, the Soviets had invited Afghan government and Army officials to a variety of social events on the evening of December 27. The Soviet minister of communications, for example, hosted a reception for Afghan communications officials in Kabul. After most of the guests had arrived, the minister gave a signal, and his athletic-looking aides detained them. At another celebration honoring officers of the Afghan capital garrison, Soviet agents delivered an ideological pep talk, then served their visitors beer and vodka. At 6:30 p.m., the Russian hosts drifted toward the exits, suddenly slamming and locking the doors. These guests also became prisoners.

As these events unfolded, one group of Spetsnaz troops set out in the cold darkness for Radio Kabul. Those slated to capture President Amin slipped into Afghan uniforms, climbed aboard trucks and light armored vehicles bearing the markings of the Afghan army, and headed for Tajbeg Palace, where the president was living.

Amin had moved to the palace less than a week earlier. It lay several miles southeast of the capital among a collection of buildings known as the Darulaman complex, which also contained the headquarters of the Afghan army. Why Amin vacated his customary residence in Kabul is unclear. He might have done so at the suggestion of the Russians, or he might have thought he would be safer outside the city. He had been wounded in one of Taraki's attempts to assassinate him and felt so threatened by Communist conspiracies, foreign and domestic, that he had planned to start an anti-Communist bloodbath on December 29. Darulaman was stoutly defended. The raiders would have to penetrate a thicket of barbed wire and overcome eight T-55 tanks of the Afghan army as well as a number of other armored vehicles that guarded the palace.

A convoy of trucks and BMD fighting vehicles carried the Spetsnaz troops. In command was Colonel Bayerenov, head of the KGB's terrorist training school. A force of perhaps three battalions of airborne troops accompanied the commandos. Altogether, nearly 2,000 men were heading for the palace.

Like most military operations, however, this one would not go quite as planned. The raiders first ran into trouble at an Afghan army checkpoint on the road to Darulaman. Instead of passing the vehicles through, Afghan soldiers advanced to inspect them. Determined not to risk further delay or even discovery, the Soviet commandos acted. Throwing back the canvas flaps of the lead truck, they triggered submachine-gun blasts that chopped the inquisitive Afghans to the ground. Then the convoy moved on.

As the raiders approached the palace, they were expecting to find Amin incapacitated. His well-deserved reputation as a fighter had led Soviet planners to order the cook to drug everybody's lunch. That way, the president's switching of dishes and drinks would go for naught. The plan almost worked. As the drug took effect, even Amin's Russian physician fell into a deep slumber at the table. But the president's wife, feeling ill, had not taken the noon meal, and she became alarmed when the diners all dozed off immediately after they had eaten. In a panic, she summoned Afghan doctors, who rushed in and frantically pumped out the stomachs of the household. When the Soviets arrived at the palace about 7:00 p.m., Amin was groggy but conscious.

At the entrance to the palace, one of the BMDs rammed into the brier-patch barbed wire surrounding the building. Instead of breaking through, the vehicle stalled, hung up in twisted metal and partially blocking the driveway. Shooting erupted as the Soviets succeeded in opening a gap in the wire. At this point, Colonel Bayerenov leaped from his vehicle and dashed into the palace with his Spetsnaz team, ordering the troops who remained outside to let none of the occupants of the palace escape. Other Soviet elements engaged Afghan security forces protecting the building.

Upon entering, some of the attackers shouted in Farsi, Afghanistan's official language: "Amin, where are you? We have come to help you." Responding to the apparent offer of aid amid the din of firing, Amin's eldest son ran forward yelling, "This way! Come this way!" Spetsnaz troopers gunned him down and ran over his body.

The assault force kicked in doors, tossed grenades into rooms, then bounded inside, their rifles and submachine guns blazing. Yet Amin's guards fought hard. At one point, a successful outcome seemed so in doubt that Bayerenov raced to the palace entrance to summon reinforcements. As he rushed outside, the KGB colonel fell victim to his own instructions. Caught in a Soviet cross fire, he died in the courtyard.

Ultimately, superior Soviet numbers and firepower prevailed. Amin was slain in a bar in the palace. All his family, his guards, and even his Russian doctor died, too. Only one defender is known to have survived the massacre, an Afghan captain trained in the Soviet Union. "The Spetsnaz," he later recounted, "used weapons equipped with silencers and shot down their adversaries like professional killers."

If the plan had been to capture Amin alive with as little fuss as possible, it went seriously awry. Not only was the president dead, but the raiders had suffered casualties in the bloody action amounting to some twenty-five killed and more than 200 wounded. When the Soviets took their dead to the airport the next day, one casket received honors appropriate to a Soviet general officer. Later, an unusual obituary appeared on the back pages of *Pravda*, tersely announcing the death on December 28 of Lieutenant General Viktor Paputin, First Deputy Minister of Internal Affairs, an agency

A relic of conflicts past guards the rear of Tajbeg Palace, part of a complex built near Kabul after the First World War. The burned-out window on the upper floor *(inset)* marks the room where Afghan president Hafizullah Amin was slain.

more commonly known as the MVD. Although there has never been confirmation, it is likely the general was one of those mortally wounded.

Despite all of the problems at the palace, the December 1979 takeover of Afghanistan was accomplished with breathtaking speed. In less than eighteen hours, the Soviets paralyzed an army, spiked a national communications system, eliminated one chief of state, and installed another. Now the Afghan Communists could fight a civil war with Soviet muscle as well as advice behind them.

Within hours of Amin's assassination, Marshal Sergei L. Sokolov's 40th Army began rolling into the country. During the early morning hours of December 28, combat vehicles of the 360th Motorized Rifle Division rapidly rolled down from Uzbekistan and crossed into Afghanistan over recently assembled pontoon bridges spanning the Amu Darya River. The 201st Division quickly followed. At the same time, a heavy-armor force of T-54 and T-64 tanks tightened the grip on the vital Salang Pass Tunnel, paving the way for a rush toward Kabul. In the west, the 66th Motorized Rifle Division and the 357th Soviet Division roared south along Soviet-built highways from Turkmenistan, aiming toward Herāt. As dawn broke, MiG-21s and MiG-23s screamed through the skies.

Later that day, the Soviets once again installed a new puppet president in Afghanistan. Babrak Karmal, a longtime KGB agent who was deemed more reliable than Amin or Taraki, began his

official duties by dusting off a "Treaty of Friendship, Good Neighborliness, and Cooperation" signed with Moscow in 1978 by then-president Taraki. Karmal used it to call for Soviet intervention well after troops had flooded the country. The work of Spetsnaz in Afghanistan appeared to be finished. Their numbers were reduced as the regular army grappled with the Mujahedin in the mountainous countryside. In time, however, those efforts would bog down, and Spetsnaz would return to the land of the Khyber Pass in ever-increasing numbers in a last-ditch but ultimately fruitless effort to turn the tide against the jihad.

The Spetsnaz assault on Tajbeg Palace stands as an example—albeit a poorly planned and bloody one—of a brute-force approach to special operations. Precision and discretion were of secondary importance, at most. Spetsnaz was a cudgel, swung hard enough to ensure that Afghanistan's head of state had no chance of survival.

Russian troops and armored vehicles, delivered by air transport, crowd the Kabul airport in early January 1980 at the height of the invasion of Afghanistan by Soviet forces. In a four-day period, some 350 flights landed in the Kabul area. The inset shows an IL-76 jet, comparable in capacity to the U.S. Air Force's C-141 Starlifter.

The very opposite approach can be exemplified by another mission involving a head of state. This one, occurring only seven months after the Afghanistan overthrow, involved Britain's 22d Special Air Service Regiment. The scene was the Republic of the Gambia, a sliver of a nation along the Gambia River in West Africa. What the SAS accomplished there was done so subtly that the British government ever after has been able to deny any role in the struggle. For all practical purposes, the SAS was invisible.

On August 1, 1981, Lieutenant Colonel Michael Rose, commanding officer of the 22d, was hiking with his two children in the Welsh hill country. The regiment had been on alert for a week. A number of Commonwealth heads of state had been in London, attending the wedding of Prince Charles to Lady Diana Spencer. The gathering of notables presented a number of opportunities for terrorists, so the SAS had made ready to deploy on a moment's notice from their base in Hereford, about an hour's helicopter flight from the capital. With London returning to normal, Rose had arranged some time off. True vacations were rare for Rose. Even now he wore an electronic beeper on his belt, which interrupted this much-anticipated interlude with an urgent summons. He was to call his headquarters as quickly as he could reach a telephone.

Major Ian Crooke, the 22d's executive officer, took Rose's call. From Crooke, the commander learned that the small nation of Gambia, a former British colony, was in the throes of a coup d'état. Launched two days earlier, it coincided with the absence of the nation's president, Sir Dawda Jawara, who was representing his country at the royal wedding. Crooke reported that Jawara had asked British Prime Minister Margaret Thatcher for help. Senegal, Gambia's neighbor, had already sent troops to combat the rebels, but Thatcher agreed to dispatch a couple of SAS men to the scene. Strictest secrecy was to be observed. Even this modest response, if it became public, could open her government to charges of renewed imperialism in Africa.

Rose was admired throughout Britain as the commando leader who had freed twenty hostages in a brilliant eleven-minute rescue operation at the Iranian embassy in London the preceding spring. Speaking on the telephone with Crooke, he was inclined to take the assignment himself. Not only was he the boss, but he had a reputation for being almost prescient at making quick decisions without benefit of all the facts, a skill that might well prove to be useful in Gambia. Moreover, the prime minister herself had called on the regiment. Its reputation was at stake. But the commander would have to be picked up by helicopter. Someone would have to come to get Rose's children and his car. All of that would take several hours, and in these situations, minutes could be crucial. So Rose told Crooke to pick a man to go with him and get to Gambia on the first available plane.

Gambia is almost completely surrounded by Senegal, a former French colony. Only 4,000 square miles in area, it is among the smallest nations in Africa and one of the continent's few democracies. In 1980, its average annual income—only $210 per capita—was on the decline because the local cash crop, peanuts, had fared

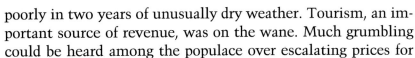

poorly in two years of unusually dry weather. Tourism, an important source of revenue, was on the wane. Much grumbling could be heard among the populace over escalating prices for rice, cooking oil, and sugar, and over the high rate of unemployment. The disaffected went about painting antigovernment slogans on walls. The president's private yacht mysteriously caught fire. For several months, his advisers had shared with him their suspicion that a coup was being planned. Jawara, however, discounted the information and flew to London for the matrimonial festivities.

Trouble in Gambia at this time automatically raised the specter of Muammar al-Qadhafi. The mercurial Libyan leader envisioned a confederation of Islamic African states under his guidance. He attracted exiled African political leaders of Marxist persuasion to the Libyan capital and plotted to reshape a number of African governments. With Libya's oil wealth, he purchased Soviet-bloc weaponry to arm his troops. He dispatched forces to shore up the brutal Ugandan president, Idi Amin. He ordered his army into Chad. He supported Polisario guerrillas fighting Morocco for control of the Western Sahara. Gambia, being 70 percent Muslim, lay within Colonel Qadhafi's fancied Islamic realm.

At 5:00 a.m. on Thursday, July 30, the coup erupted. Muscle for the attempt to overthrow Jawara was provided by Usman Bojang. A former deputy commander of Gambia's 300-man Police Field Force—a paramilitary organization charged with preserving order in the tiny country—Bojang managed to persuade or force the contingent based in the town of Bakau to join the coup. This group, which amounted to about one-third of the organization, disarmed most of the loyal police, then quickly took over the nearby transmitter for Radio Gambia and moved into Banjul, the capital. On the way, they opened the country's largest prison and distributed weapons from the police armory, not only to the inmates but to virtually anyone who happened along. Not long after daybreak, citizens and former prisoners alike began rampaging through the streets and looting shops. Soon, a free-for-all erupted. Within the first few hours of the coup, scores of bodies—policemen, criminals, and civilians—littered the streets of Banjul.

Philosophical underpinnings for the revolt were provided by the Gambian Socialist Revolutionary Party, which was headed by a

Sir Dawda Jawara, president of Gambia, stands before the residence of the Gambian high commissioner in London on July 30, 1981. In Britain to attend the wedding of Prince Charles and Lady Diana Spencer, Sir Dawda exuded confidence for photographers, even though Marxist malcontents had launched a coup against his government that very morning.

young Marxist named Kukoi Samba Sanyang. His given name was Dominique, but when he became a Communist, he changed it to Kukoi, a word in the Mandinka language, native to Gambia, that means "sweep clean." Sanyang was also among the African radicals who had sojourned in Libya.

Arriving at Radio Gambia shortly after rebel policemen seized the station, Sanyang closed the country's borders and its airport at Yundum, some fifteen miles east of Banjul. Then he proclaimed a "dictatorship of the proletariat" and charged the "bourgeois" Jawara government with corruption, injustice, and nepotism.

Very few foreigners lived in the capital. The majority resided in the nearby communities of Bakau and Fajara, where most of the tourist hotels stood. Europeans and Americans—some of them on vacation, others working in business or government capacities—mostly stayed off the streets. In some cases, rebel Gambian policemen, who saw no profit in harming such individuals, guided anxious foreigners to the residence of the United States ambassador, Larry G. Piper. The house was soon haven to 123 nervous guests, 80 of them American citizens.

On the outskirts of Banjul, along the nation's beautiful seacoast, a number of European tourists sought shelter in the Atlantic Beach Hotel. Two armed looters found their way inside, ransacked the safe, took the hotel manager hostage, and fled the building—right into the gunsights of unidentified adversaries, who shot and killed the two criminals virtually on the hotel doorstep. Hearing more firing outside, the foreigners shrank from windows. They organized watches and even posted guards, "armed" with fire extinguishers, at the hotel's entrances.

Had such stories reached the world outside Gambia, the coup would have attracted far more attention than it did. During the first day of the coup, however, Jawara was, in effect, controlling the news from London. In contact by telephone with his vice president, who had taken refuge in police headquarters in Banjul, where he was protected by loyalist troops, Jawara wisely made himself accessible to the press. By doing so, he was able to downplay events at home. As if to resume control of the government, Jawara boarded a jet bound for Dakar, capital of Senegal. Before leaving, he acknowledged that he had considered invoking a mutual assistance treaty that Gambia had signed with Senegal some fifteen years earlier to fend off external aggression. That no foreign provocateur had yet surfaced seemed to be of little concern.

Such was the situation as Rose ordered Crooke to Gambia. The major and the SAS sergeant he chose to accompany him assembled their gear: German-made Heckler & Koch submachine guns, Browning 9-mm automatic pistols, and a stock of ammunition and grenades. The first available plane happened to be an Air France commercial flight to Dakar. Although firearms can be carried in checked baggage aboard such aircraft, explosives are prohibited. By availing himself of some informal contacts within British and French military and diplomatic circles, however, Crooke managed to pass his little arsenal through customs and baggage checks and onto the plane. Dressed casually in blue jeans, the two SAS men drew no attention from their fellow travelers, among whom were many reporters and television camera crews.

The day after arriving in Senegal, Crooke encountered his first obstacle—British diplomats. With fighting going on between the rebel forces and Senegalese troops, and with a considerable number of British citizens in danger, officials in both Dakar and Banjul decided that it would only complicate their duties further if Crooke and his sergeant were to get into the act. Much preferring simply to applaud the Senegalese if the intervention succeeded or to chastise them if it failed, the diplomats forbade the major and his sergeant to proceed.

Crooke listened impassively to these instructions, then returned to the airport and began looking for the quickest way into Gambia. The major reasoned that if the prime minister had sent word to detain him, the harried British diplomats in Senegal would have said so. And with no word from Thatcher, in whose service he had come to Africa, Crooke decided to go ahead with his mission despite the remonstrations of these relatively minor officials. He resolved to hop a plane bound for Gambia's Yundum airport, where the Senegalese paratroop commander, Lieutenant Colonel Abdourahman N'Gom, had established his headquarters.

As he set about translating resolve into action, Crooke met up with Clive Lee, a hulking six-foot-six retired SAS major who was employed in Gambia as a civilian adviser to the Gambian Pioneer Corps, a division of the Field Force that trained rural youth in agricultural and construction skills. Hearing of the coup on the radio, Lee had rounded up twenty-three Pioneer Corps members, armed them, and set off for Banjul. To get there from the Pioneer Corps base in the town of Farafenni, sixty miles east of the capital, he had to cross the Gambia River. Because of the hostilities, however, the ferry had suspended operations. The imposing sight of the Briton and his platoon persuaded the captain to roust his crew and take Lee's band to the other side.

Once across the river, they made their way to Banjul, moving through mangrove swamps to avoid rebel positions along the main approach to the city. Reaching the capital on August 1, they headed for police headquarters, where they reinforced a small contingent of loyalists and barricaded nearby streets to keep the rebels at bay.

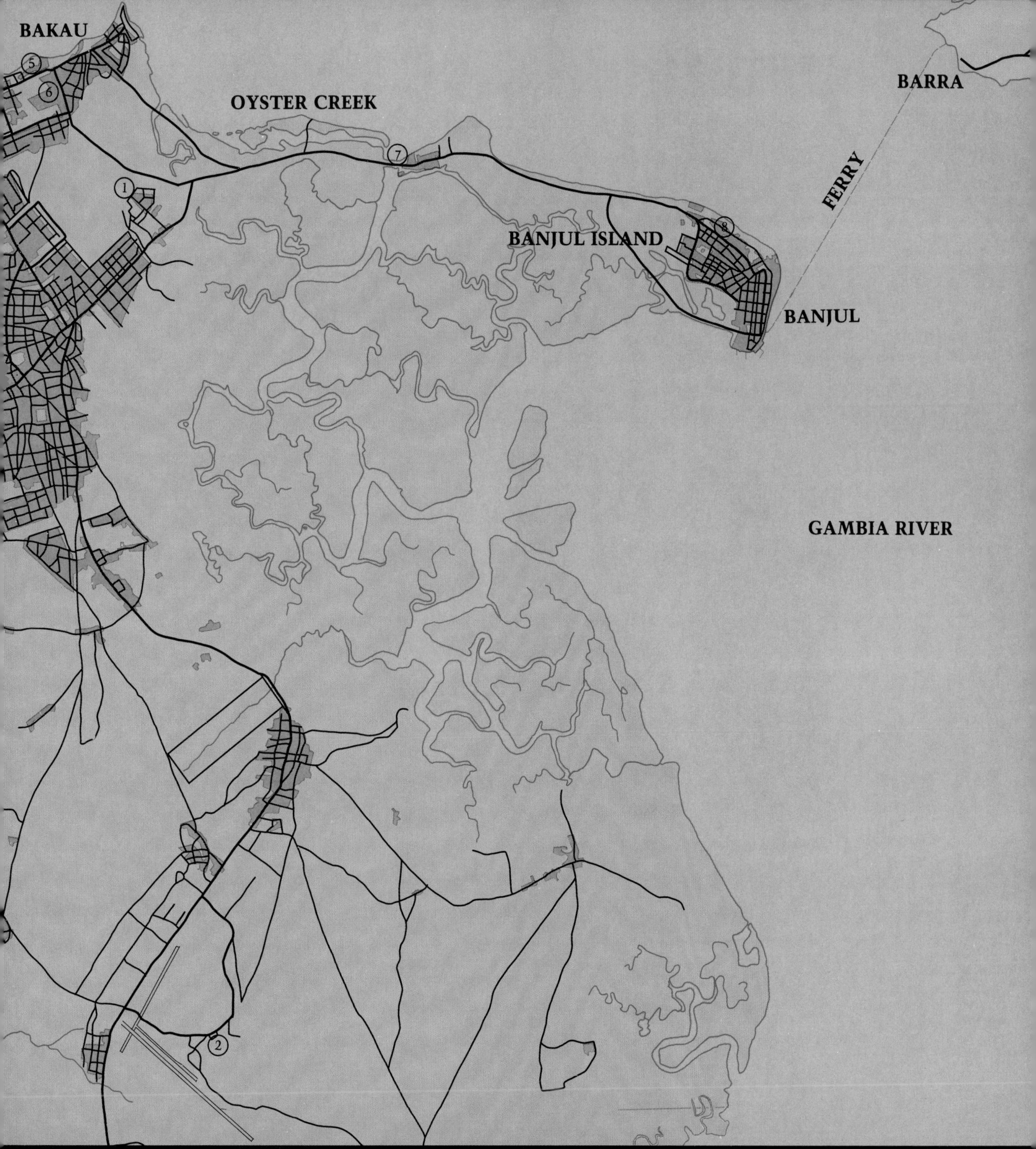

BAKAU

⑤

⑥

OYSTER CREEK

BARRA

①

FERRY

⑦

BANJUL ISLAND

⑧

BANJUL

GAMBIA RIVER

②

The Gambian revolt of 1981 started in Bakau and quickly spread to the capital city of Banjul. The rebels first seized the radio station ①, then the airport at Yundum ②. Foreigners gathered for safety at the residence of the U.S. ambassador ③ and at the Atlantic Beach Hotel ⑧.

① RADIO GAMBIA	⑤ BRITISH HIGH COMMISSION
② YUNDUM AIRPORT	⑥ POLICE FIELD FORCE COMPOUND
③ U.S. AMBASSADOR'S RESIDENCE	⑦ DENTON BRIDGE
④ MEDICAL RESEARCH CENTER	⑧ ATLANTIC BEACH HOTEL

That evening, Senegalese soldiers entered Banjul, having captured Yundum airport a day earlier after a fierce battle in which nearly half the 120 paratroops making the assault were wounded or killed. Within a few hours, the Senegalese had cleared Banjul of rebels and had gained control of Denton bridge across Oyster Creek to prevent insurgents from reentering the capital from their concentrations in Bakau and Fajara. With the route from Banjul to the airport reasonably secure, Lee had set off for the airport and Dakar.

The SAS keeps in contact with former members, so Crooke probably expected to come upon Lee at some point. It is even conceivable that Lee had word that Crooke was en route and hurried to Dakar to meet him. In any event, the Pioneer Corps adviser was quickly recruited. Introducing themselves to one of N'Gom's officers, the three Britons had little trouble finding a space on an airplane bound for Gambia.

Helping the Gambian government put down the 1981 uprising, tough-looking Senegalese paratroopers and sharpshooters search for rebel guerrillas at a Gambian military compound. Before Senegal became independent, it was a French colony. Its soldiers, well known for their superb training and discipline, were instructed by the French and fought alongside them in Vietnam.

On arrival, they found the situation little changed. Although N'Gom continued to strengthen his forces in Gambia and occasionally traded shots with the rebels, the military situation had reached an impasse. His troops were stalled outside Bakau because Sanyang had taken more than a hundred hostages. The most valuable captives were Lady Chilel N'Jie—one of President Jawara's two wives—and a number of his children. In addition, Sanyang held several members of the Gambian cabinet. And although N'Gom had wrested Radio Gambia from Sanyang's rebels (the transmitter lay between the airport and the bridge), the coup leader had commandeered a mobile transmitter from which Lady Chilel appealed almost hysterically to Senegal, announcing that the hostages would be executed unless the paratroops withdrew. Sanyang repeated the threat himself. "I shall kill the whole lot," he warned, "and thereafter stand to fight the Senegalese."

On August 5, Crooke decided to make a reconnaissance. The blue-jeans-clad SAS officer and his two associates slipped forward of Senegalese outposts and set out afoot. The weather was hot; during August in Gambia, temperatures routinely exceed 90° F.

Three Britons carrying submachine guns could hardly escape notice in Fajara, but the outing was not as dangerous as it might seem. Although there was always the chance that an encounter with an armed insurgent could end in gunfire, the rebels did not seem inclined to harm Europeans. Furthermore, Crooke observed an unmilitary laxity among the troops manning rebel positions. Unknown to both Crooke and the outside world, Bojang had been killed during the second day of the coup. His absence and the resulting lack of leadership probably accounted for the apparent decline in rebel vigilance. Crooke's sortie confirmed that the insurgents were now capable of little more than token resistance against the well-trained Senegalese troops.

Crooke persuaded N'Gom to begin an advance on Fajara and Bakau the same day. The British officer and his companions accompanied a contingent of Senegalese troops along the hot byways of the suburbs. Peter Fenlon, a British engineer employed by an American crane company, saw the party when they appeared at his hotel in Fajara. "Ten Senegalese troops and a British Army officer arrived at the hotel," the engineer recalled. The officer, probably

Clive Lee, wore khakis with no insignia. "With him were two men who I can only describe as the most vicious-looking professionals I have ever seen." Upon being told that rebels were hiding along a creek near the beach, the pair set off to find them. "There was sporadic violent gunfire," said Fenlon, "then the two men walked calmly back to our hotel."

A U.S. aid worker at the American embassy was one of the foreigners who had taken refuge in Ambassador Larry Piper's house. It was early afternoon, he remembered, when a lookout they had posted announced that soldiers were coming up the hill. "The house," said the aid worker later, "was on a bluff sloping to the beach. I went out and saw a wave of Senegalese come running up the hill in full camouflage-type gear led by three whites, one of whom had on an Australian hat, khaki shorts, and a knife strapped to his leg. It was literally like living in a movie." After ascertaining that everyone was all right and leaving behind a dozen or so paratroops for security, the party disappeared.

Arriving at the British high commissioner's offices, Crooke learned that armed rebel guards had escorted President Jawara's wife and her four ailing children—one of them an infant of only five weeks—to a British clinic the day before. Doctors at this tropical-disease research facility, which stood only a block or two from the high commissioner's office, treated the children and advised her to bring them back within twenty-four hours.

That interval had passed, and now Lady Chilel had returned for follow-up care. This information came by way of a telephone call to the high commissioner from the British physician attending the children. The official told the doctor that armed SAS men would be there within minutes, and Crooke and his two companions quickly headed for the hospital.

Hearing that help was on the way, the doctor began to draw out his treatment. The wily physician even convinced the woman's armed escorts that they were frightening his other patients and persuaded them to put their guns out of sight.

As Crooke approached the hospital, he noticed two armed guards posted at the entrance. Handing his submachine gun to his companions, the major gave them time to circle behind the guards, then walked up to the pair and distracted them in conversation as the other two SAS men crept up from the rear. It is difficult to imagine what Crooke could have said or how devious a plan he might have formulated in order to draw the guards' attention away from his accomplices. The SAS is mute on the topic, following the lead of the British and Gambian governments in their steadfast refusal to acknowledge that Great Britain had sent any military assistance at all. But whatever Crooke's ruse, it worked. The two guards froze when they felt gun muzzles at the backs of their heads.

Leaving the captives in the hands of his able assistants, Crooke slipped inside the clinic. He surprised Lady Chilel's weaponless escorts as they watched the children being treated and promptly took them prisoner. After conducting the president's wife and children to the high commissioner's office, Crooke and his party retreated to N'Gom's headquarters at the airport.

A day earlier, Senegalese troops, who now numbered about 1,500, had found and destroyed the mobile transmitter that Sanyang had been using. Although Sanyang himself escaped, he was no longer a factor. With the silencing of its leaders, the coup's backbone was broken. Yet many hostages remained under rebel guns at a police

Tracking down defeated rebels, members of the Gambian police department—most of whom remained loyal to Jawara—batter down a door in an effort to find a suspected insurgent. Although many of the rebels shed their military uniforms to avoid being identified, more than 1,000 men were arrested in the roundup.

barracks, and disorganized bands of turncoat policemen and criminals had to be rounded up.

N'Gom paced his advance slowly. Panic among the rebels might cause them to begin killing their prisoners. They had nearly done so a few days earlier, when a policeman who had been forced against his better judgment to join the coup began shooting some of the rebel guards. He was killed in a trice, but his brave act seemed to thwart the planned execution. The Senegalese paratroops edged up to one side of the barracks, leaving several exits unguarded for the rebels to flee. After a tense hour or so, the hostages walked free, and the insurgents dispersed, to be captured later.

It was all over. After eight days of rebellion and perhaps as many as 1,000 deaths, President Jawara was once again the unchallenged and elected head of the Gambian government. In Banjul, he posed for reporters, hugged his baby son, and pronounced: "I'm relieved and happy." However, when he was asked about the Europeans his wife Chilel reported as having rescued her and the children, he stonewalled, implying that she and any others making such a claim must have been mistaken.

Crooke stayed on in Gambia only long enough to satisfy himself that British citizens would be safe. A number of whites besides Peter Fenlon had observed him and his two companions carrying submachine guns, but the SAS men refused to reveal their identity or acknowledge their connection with the British Army. To a group of happy Canadians, they admitted being British, but not SAS. "We don't say anything about that" was their reply.

To make Jawara's political recovery as easy as possible, all official comment about the countercoup and rescue was reserved for African governments. The only confirmation of the SAS presence came from a Senegalese officer, who told reporters that SAS personnel had indeed participated in restoring order. The British government has remained silent to this day.

Kukoi Sanyang was eventually arrested in the neighboring country of Guinea-Bissau, but the socialist government there later released him, despite Gambian requests for his extradition. Senegalese troops captured more than a hundred of the rebels and convicts, seven of whom were ultimately condemned to death. Libya was never connected directly with the coup attempt.

Trick helps soldiers free Gambian leader's family

Maggie orders SAS to rescue

By JOHN BURNS and JAMES DAVIES

A DRAMATIC rescue of the Gambian President's family from rebels was carried out by the SAS on Mrs Thatcher's orders, it was reported last night.

And in his capital of Banjul, President Sir Dawda Jawara hugged his baby son and said: "I'm very relieved and happy."

Moslem Sir Dawda was in London with his No 2 wife for Prince Charles's wedding when marxists staged a coup in the ex-British Colony in West Africa and seized his No 1 wife and eight children as hostages.

THE PLEA

The President—knowing the reputation of the Special Air Service from its action in the Iranian Embassy siege in London—appealed to the Prime Minister for help.

The Government acted swiftly—and as the uprising developed into a clash with troops from neighbouring Senegal, a major and a sergeant of the SAS slipped across the Gambia River into rebel lines.

The President's senior wife, Lady Thielai, was held with the eight children in a compound outside Banjul. Conditions, she said later, were "very difficult" and she was constantly threatened with death.

Four of the children, including a five-week-old baby, were ill—and the chance of rescue came when the mother was allowed to take her family under guard to a clinic run by a Briton, Dr Brian Greenwood.

The SAS men, with Senegalese commandos, set up a trap. The rebels escorting Lady Thielai were asked not to frighten patients and to leave their guns outside the clinic—and they were promptly seized. The President's family was whisked to safety by helicopter.

THE TERROR

The other four children were still held prisoner along with 22 people—but yesterday when Senegalese troops raced to the compound the rebels fled and the hostages were saved.

Their days of terror were described by 16-year-old Lamin Faal, a diplomat's son, crowded into a hut with other youngsters.

He said one rebel, a policeman, killed five of his own men for threatening the hostages—but was himself shot the same day.

And shortly afterwards the leader of the uprising, Kukoi Sanyang, disappeared from the compound.

THE HOLIDAY

Meanwhile 25 Britons—several of them on a package holiday and including six children—were freed from Banjul's Atlantic Hotel.

Before they left for home last night Mr Steve Grimes, 26, from Lee, London, said: "There was shooting all around the hotel for several days, and a lot of looting, especially after the rebels opened the prison. The Wadner Beach Hotel was ransacked. A looter at our hotel was shot dead."

Continued on Back P. Col 3

How the SAS freed tourists

By PETER DOBBIE

A BRITISH ENGINEER, trapped by rebels during the abortive coup in The Gambia, described yesterday how two jean-clad Special Air Service soldiers, each armed with two pistols and a sub-machine gun, freed himself and 40 other people from a beachside hotel at the height of the fighting.

Mr Peter Fenlon, 34, from Manchester, experienced a terrifying week of death threats, street fighting and looting at Bakau, 12 miles from the capital of Banjul, which ended with the arrival of the SAS and Senegalese troops.

Mr Fenlon, a senior engineer with the American-owned Grove Crane company, said he believed that the same SAS men were responsible for freeing the wife and four children of Sir Dawda Jarawa, the Gambian President.

Mr Fenlon, who flew to The Gambia on Royal Wedding day to inspect two cranes, described his meeting with the British soldiers.

"On Wednesday morning, Senegalese troops arrived at Bakau in force," he said. "They had obviously been through one hell of a battle with the rebels and I counted 16 bullet holes in one truck. Later that morning 10 Senegalese troops and a British Army officer arrived at the hotel. He wore a khaki shirt and trousers without any insignia or rank identification. His manner was proper and very Sandhurst and he had complete control of the situation.

"With him were two men who I can only describe as two of the most vicious-looking professionals I have ever seen. They each wore hard guns, one on each hip, and carried small, compact, machine guns. They were dressed casually in jeans and blue check shirts. From a distance you could hardly tell they were armed.

"I asked one of them how long he had been serving with the Senegalese Army. He replied: 'I am British—I am definitely not in the Senegalese Army.'

"I said: 'It is nice to see the SAS has arrived.' He smiled and replied: 'We don't say anything about that.'"

Mr Fenlon and other guests and local residents who crowded into the hotel for safety told the soldiers that rebels were still hiding in a creek close to the beach.

"The two SAS men went off towards the creek," Mr Fenlon said. "I can't say whether Senegalese troops went with them. There was sporadic violent gunfire for about 90 minutes. Then the two men walked calmly back to our hotel, I later heard that they were involved in the release of the President's family."

Mr Fenlon criticised officials at the British consulate in Bakau who, he claimed, had done little to help Britons and other foreign nationals trapped in the town. He was told he could leave aboard a RAF Hercules but would first have to sign forms agreeing to pay for the flight and any interest incurred through default of payment.

The Foreign Office rejected suggestions that British officials in The Gambia had been unhelpful.

An official confirmed that those who had been brought out by RAF Hercules had either paid for their flights in cash or signed an indemnity promising to pay at a later date.

The official said: "There were no commercial flights and we feel we acted quickly in getting people out."

The Ministry of Defence said yesterday that Hercules aircraft would continue to ferry British nationals from The Gambia daily.

The SAS operation in Gambia was a gem of its genre: situations in which a few skilled and confident soldiers can influence an event far out of proportion to their numbers—and depart leaving almost no trace of their presence. Crooke was so discreet that his name was not linked with the episode for almost seven years. The British government, by refusing to admit involvement, handled the affair as an African problem, solved by Africans. Partly as a result of London's smooth statecraft, neither Libya nor the Soviet Union made political gains in West Africa during the early 1980s.

The success of the action, however, hinged in large measure on Crooke's initiative and good judgment. That he had a lot of help is undisputed. It came partly in the form of militarily incompetent coup makers and partly from the presence of the Senegalese. N'Gom's troops supplied the manpower needed to fight rebels who were disinclined to surrender and to maintain security in areas that had been swept clean. Nonetheless, Crooke was the one who tipped the balance. He chose to ignore the restrictions placed on him by British diplomats and acted as he believed the prime minister wished. Had he been wrong, he would have no doubt suffered severe consequences. But there were also penalties for inaction. An SAS officer is expected to act boldly, and Crooke could not face his commander with the lame excuse that timid envoys had prevented an obvious course of action. ✹✹✹

111

The Tools of a Deadly Trade

The Green Berets, part of the U.S. Army's Special Operations Forces, have a unique collection of weapons and other gear at their disposal. Some of the arsenal is made in America, but it also includes equipment from the NATO allies, from the Soviet Union and its satellites, and from China, Finland, Sweden, Israel, and other countries.

Foreign weapons offer several advantages. If seen or captured, they and their ammunition would not immediately betray an American presence. In hostile territory, a U.S. team could reload with captured ammunition. Moreover, the distinctive sound of an indigenous rifle might deceive a foe into thinking that its own troops were firing.

To qualify as a weapons specialist, a Special Forces soldier must be on intimate terms with at least eighty different types. The final exam is the "pile test," in which an unspecified number of unidentified weapons are stripped and their parts piled in a heap. The trainee has to identify the weapons, sort the parts, and put them back together in firing order—all to the tick of an instructor's stopwatch.

Such skills are critical, for the Green Berets must be prepared to practice their craft under all circumstances, anywhere on earth. Their primary roles are to operate behind enemy lines, raise makeshift armies of locals, and advise foreign governments in the art of defeating armed insurrection. They also conduct long-range reconnaissance behind enemy lines and mount swift, surgical strikes against enemy installations.

Each mission requires a different mix of firearms and other gear. As guerrilla fighters and counterguerrilla advisers, the Green Berets have found that the best weapons for the job are simple, reliable, and—most important—readily available. At the other end of the spectrum, reconnaissance or strike missions can involve the highest level of technology, including a high-powered sniper rifle that fires explosive, incendiary bullets. From half a mile away, one round can send up an ammunition dump, shoot down a helicopter, or reduce an antiaircraft radar to splinters of glass and metal.

Buttstock extended for use, the AKMS assault rifle measures thirty-five inches. Folded, it shrinks to a compact twenty-eight inches, a great convenience to a parachuting Green Beret. The weapon is easily recognized by the prominent tube, bending toward the top of the barrel, that channels propellant gases rearward to operate the bolt. The AKMS fires a 7.62-mm cartridge that is somewhat longer and more powerful than the cartridge fired by the M-16, America's equivalent weapon. When it is operated in full-automatic mode, the AKMS assault rifle shoots 600 rounds per minute, fast enough to expend a standard 30-cartridge magazine in just three seconds.

Using the Weapons of Friend and Foe

Both an assault rifle and a small submachine gun are capable of automatically firing one shot at a time or round after round as long as there are bullets in the magazine. Each excels in situations where the other is only adequate, yet in some instances the two types may be used interchangeably.

The assault-rifle concept, which originated in Germany in the early 1940s, is embodied in the Soviet Union's Kalashnikov AKMS shown above. Like all assault rifles, this one, descended from the AK-47 of Vietnam renown, fires a cartridge of only moderate power. The smaller charge sacrifices range but reduces recoil. The resulting weapon is relatively easy to hold on the target when fired as an automatic, hand-held machine gun. Like the heavier AK-47, the folding-stock AKMS is simple and reliable. With liberal clearances between its few moving parts, the AKMS will function after being buried in mud or sand.

The Heckler & Koch MP5K submachine gun, shown at far right, was designed in the mid-1960s. Some thirty-five nations issue various models of the German MP5 to their armies, often in preference to the Israeli Uzi, a weapon long the standard of excellence. Known to the Green Berets as the "room-broom," the stubby, stockless gun is easy to conceal. It is most effective for sweeping bursts of fire in close quarters, but a superior sight and firing mechanism make the MP5K accurate at ranges up to seventy-five meters.

Only 12.8 inches long, the diminutive Heckler & Koch MP5K submachine gun gets off a ripping 900 rounds per minute in full-automatic mode. The MP5K's 9-mm Parabellum NATO cartridge is the same one used in many semiautomatic handguns. To conserve ammunition, the MP5K can be set by means of a lever to fire one shot at a time or to loose a three-round burst with each pull of the trigger.

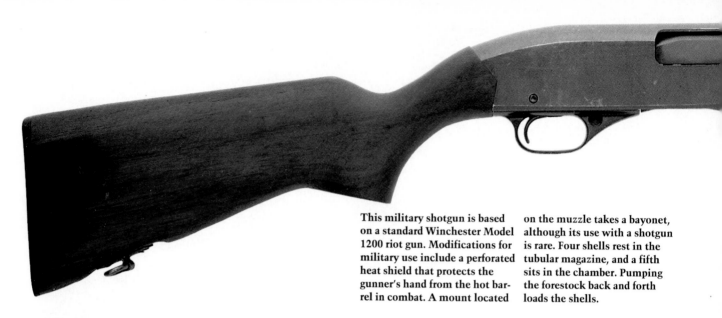

This military shotgun is based on a standard Winchester Model 1200 riot gun. Modifications for military use include a perforated heat shield that protects the gunner's hand from the hot barrel in combat. A mount located on the muzzle takes a bayonet, although its use with a shotgun is rare. Four shells rest in the tubular magazine, and a fifth sits in the chamber. Pumping the forestock back and forth loads the shells.

Versatility from an Old Standby

Probing ten or more meters in front of his teammates, the point man on patrol is in a vulnerable position. In a sudden encounter with the enemy, when the first shot must count, nothing beats a blast of buckshot from a 12-gauge shotgun.

The Winchester Model 1200 shotgun above is a modified version of a police riot gun. Semiautomatic shotguns are popular among hunters, but they are undependable in combat, too likely to jam in damp, dirty, or frigid conditions. The Green Berets prefer guns with a simple pump action. A skilled shooter can fire all five rounds from the Winchester within a few seconds.

An effective 12-gauge combat load contains nine pellets of No. 00 buckshot, each about one-third of an inch in diameter. In flight, the pellets spread out until, at twenty-five meters, the shot pattern covers a circle a little wider than a man's chest. Smaller shot is sometimes used, sacrificing punch in favor of more pellets—twenty-seven No. 4 pellets fit into a 12-gauge shell. However, clothing can stop the quarter-inch balls at ranges beyond thirty meters.

Buckshot is by no means the only load available. A wide variety of munitions can transform the shotgun into a versatile, multipurpose weapon, as illustrated at far right.

Special Shells for Special Missions

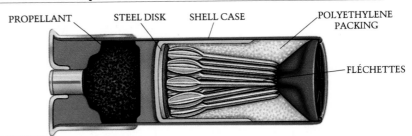

PROPELLANT · STEEL DISK · SHELL CASE · POLYETHYLENE PACKING · FLÉCHETTES

A SWARM OF DARTS

The effective range of the shotgun is increased from 50 meters to 300 meters by this round, which contains twenty steel darts called fléchettes. Packed in granulated polyethylene called grek, the fléchettes are bundled in a conical shape to reduce dispersion, and an extrapowerful charge drives a steel disk that gives them all a uniform push. The fléchettes can penetrate a steel helmet at 300 meters but are easily deflected by dense undergrowth, making the round best for open areas.

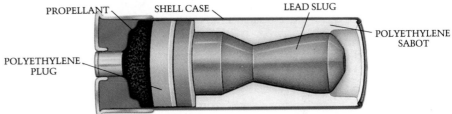

PROPELLANT · SHELL CASE · LEAD SLUG · POLYETHYLENE SABOT · POLYETHYLENE PLUG

A SLUGGING SHELL

All of the shotgun's power is concentrated in this hardened lead slug, which can penetrate a cast-iron engine block at 100 meters or blow a heavy door off its hinges. The slug is encased in a polyethylene sleeve, called a sabot, which seals the shotgun bore so that no propellant gases escape around the slug when fired. The sleeve also centers the slug in the barrel for riflelike accuracy out to 150 meters. The sabot divides into halves that fall away after exiting the muzzle.

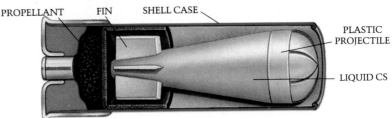

PROPELLANT · FIN · SHELL CASE · PLASTIC PROJECTILE · LIQUID CS

A TEAR-GAS BOMB

A plastic bomblet in this shell contains liquid CS tear gas. The projectile penetrates thin barriers such as car windows and paneled wood doors. As it punches through such obstacles—or smashes against more substantial ones—the bomblet bursts, atomizing the CS liquid. In less than thirty seconds, a room twelve feet square becomes uninhabitable. Fins spin the bomblet in flight to stabilize it, making the shell accurate enough to hit doors and windows fifty meters away.

Double-Barreled Covering Fire

To deal with well-entrenched defenders, troop carriers, or other lightly armored vehicles, or even to break off an engagement and retreat with minimum casualties, a Special Forces team needs more than shotguns and assault rifles. One team member might even the odds in such situations by attaching an M-203 grenade launcher to an M-16. With a 40-mm bore, the launcher accepts all manner of special-purpose ammunition: fragmentation grenades, smoke bombs, tear and nausea gas, high-explosive antitank (HEAT) rounds, parachute flares, one filled with buckshot, an incendiary round, and others. A skilled grenadier can slam a round through a window at a distance of 150 meters or keep the enemy's head down from as far away as 400 meters.

The weapon's ability to launch a half-pound object a great distance with acceptable recoil comes from an unusual propulsion method—the high-low pressure system. Pulling the trigger ignites a small cup of propellant in the cartridge case. High-pressure gas jets through vents into a surrounding low-pressure chamber. When the pressure there becomes high enough, the grenade is launched, separating from its cartridge case with a loud *bloop*, giving the weapon its nickname—the "bloop tube." The tube's rifling spins the shell at 3,700 rpm both to improve accuracy and to arm the round, which is equipped with a centrifugally activated fuze.

Shells to Pierce Armor and Light Up the Night

The M-433 cartridge *(below, left)* is both an antiarmor round and a fragmentation grenade. On impact, a fuze detonates a shaped charge, which has a conical face that projects a high-pressure jet of hot gas capable of burning a hole through two inches of steel armor. Shrapnel from the fragmentation liner can kill anyone within fifteen feet. A parachute flare *(below, right)* reaches 200 meters into the air to provide illumination or a signal visible from three miles. Five seconds after launch, a charge ejects the flare, which for forty seconds burns as brightly as a helicopter searchlight.

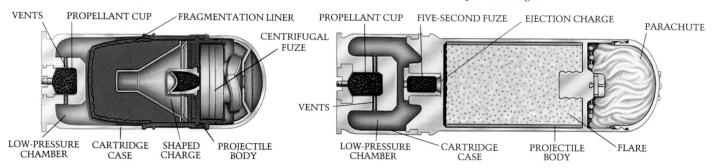

VENTS PROPELLANT CUP FRAGMENTATION LINER CENTRIFUGAL FUZE PROPELLANT CUP FIVE-SECOND FUZE EJECTION CHARGE PARACHUTE

LOW-PRESSURE CHAMBER CARTRIDGE CASE SHAPED CHARGE PROJECTILE BODY VENTS LOW-PRESSURE CHAMBER CARTRIDGE CASE PROJECTILE BODY FLARE

The M-203 grenade launcher fits beneath the barrel of an M-16A2 rifle. Together, the weapons weigh eleven pounds. The rifle is a version of the Vietnam-era M-16A1, with maximum effective range boosted from 300 to 460 meters. The launcher, consisting of a 40-mm aluminum tube, trigger, and perforated metal heat shield, replaces the rifle's forestock. The switch takes about fifteen minutes. A lever on the left side releases the launcher's barrel, which slides forward for loading. The M-16's magazine acts as a handgrip when pulling the M203's trigger.

A Quick-Change Artist among Machine Guns

One of the most adaptable weapons in the Special Forces arsenal is West Germany's Heckler & Koch light machine gun. Built by the manufacturer of the MP5K submachine gun *(page 115)*, it fires 900 rounds per minute. And because it weighs only eighteen pounds—five pounds less than most light machine guns—it can be carried along on long missions.

Heckler & Koch makes this machine gun in two models, which are identical except for their ammunition-feed systems. The HK11A1, shown above, accepts a 30-round magazine and is more suitable for offensive operations. For the sustained fire that is necessary to fend off an attack, the HK21A1, fed from a box of 100 belted cartridges, is the appropriate choice.

Both weapons can be swiftly adapted to fire a variety of Allied and East Bloc car-tridges, an unusual feature for any kind of firearm. In a few minutes, the gunner can replace the barrel, bolt, and feed mechanism, configuring the machine gun to accept one of three rounds. Each has merits and limitations. NATO's small 5.56-mm round is restricted in useful range to about 500 meters but generates low recoil. NATO's heavier 7.62-mm cartridge delivers a heftier punch and has double the range, but it produces a bone-rattling kick on full automatic. The Soviet 7.62-mm round also has the same range as the 5.56-mm cartridge but has a heavier bullet. On a long, arduous mission, the deciding factors may be size and weight. If the gunner carries ten pounds of ammunition, he can have 384 of the 5.56-mm cartridges, 277 of the midsize Soviet type, or 187 of the full-power NATO rounds.

Heckler & Koch light machine guns such as the HK11A1 *(above)* are forty inches long. Bipod legs, hinged near the muzzle, tuck under the barrel when they are not in use. Similarly, a spring-loaded carrying handle above the magazine folds aside for shooting. Buttstock and barrel are removable for parachuting with the gun stored in a backpack. To exchange an overheated barrel, the gunner first squeezes the thumb-activated release of an insulating plastic handle. He then uses the handle to rotate the barrel counterclockwise, push it forward, and withdraw it through the opening in the right side of the gun. He reverses the steps to install a cool barrel. The whole operation takes only two seconds to complete—less than the amount of time needed to load a fresh magazine.

The Ultimate Sniper Rifle

A sniper and his spotter must be as patient as hunters, lying hidden for hours or even days waiting for a target to come within range. The closer the quarry must be, the longer the wait, the greater the likelihood that the sniper will not even get to shoot, and the sharper the danger if he does.

At normal ranges of around 300 meters, an alert enemy is certain to hear the report of the rifle and may see the muzzle flash. Even at 500 meters, the sniper team is at risk of discovery. At 800 meters and beyond—half a mile or more—a sniper team can begin to feel more secure, but hitting a target at such distances is a difficult feat of marksmanship.

Nonetheless, U.S. Special Forces have a sniper rifle that can reach out more than twice as far. It is the Haskins M500, which is custom-made in limited numbers for Green Beret snipers. The weapon, named for the Arkansas gunsmith who builds it, fires a powerful .50-caliber round originally made for a heavy machine gun. Fitted with a ten-power telescopic sight and placed in the hands of a practiced marksman, this unique firearm can hit a target the size of a garbage can from 2,000 meters, a distance of a mile and a quarter.

The bullet arrives before the sound of the gun, which at such a distance is so faint that it is likely to go unnoticed. The demoralized enemy sees and hears nothing—except for the devastating effects of the bullet.

A Small Package of Destruction

This .50-caliber sniper round is primarily intended to knock out vehicles and weapons. It can shatter a tank's thermal gunsight or cripple an aircraft engine. A huge charge sends the 1.5-ounce bullet out the muzzle with five times the energy of a standard 7.62-mm NATO round. A hardened tungsten-carbide penetrator inside the projectile can pierce four-inch armor, while incendiary material in the nose will touch off stored ammunition or a fuel tank. The incendiary also detonates an explosive charge that shatters the bullet's steel fragmentation body into shrapnel.

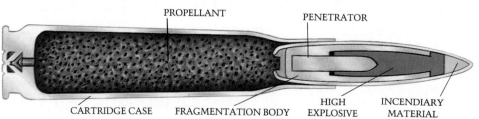

CARTRIDGE CASE PROPELLANT FRAGMENTATION BODY HIGH EXPLOSIVE PENETRATOR INCENDIARY MATERIAL

The Haskins M500, with its adjustable stock and single-shot bolt action, resembles an Olympic match rifle. Rapid fire is impossible; the bolt must be removed to load each round. But a sniper's goal is precision, not speed, and the bolt action is the most accurate firing mechanism. A fluted barrel reduces weight and speeds cooling without sacrificing the stiffness required for accuracy. Even so, the weapon weighs twenty-three pounds, making the use of a bipod necessary. A muzzle brake deflects propellant gases rearward, diminishing kick.

Catastrophe at Desert One

Headed for Tehran to free Americans held captive there, a Sea Stallion helicopter lifts from the deck of the nuclear-powered aircraft carrier *Nimitz* at sunset on April 24, 1980. Eight of the multimillion-dollar machines took part in the mission.

A chill rain fell on Tehran that morning of November 4, 1979. It was Sunday, a working day in Muslim lands, and the men and women of the U.S. embassy staff were going about their duties in the large compound on Taleghani Street in the downtown part of the city. A few months earlier, 1,000 Americans had served there. All but sixty-six had been evacuated.

These were unhappy and dangerous days in relations between the United States and Iran. In February, a popular revolt had driven the shah, Muhammad Reza Pahlavi, from the Peacock Throne of his ancestors. In the turmoil that followed, an uneasy coalition of secular politicians and fundamentalist Muslim clergymen led by the Ayatollah Khomeini had swept to power—and they all shared a searing determination to eradicate every vestige of the shah's reign. The United States, having engineered royalty's return to power in the 1950s, was singled out as the "Great Satan." In looking to the shah for stability in the Middle East, America had tended to discount his often despotic ways. Terminally ill with cancer, the exiled shah now lay in a New York City hospital, and angry mobs of students, revolutionaries, and religious fanatics paraded past the embassy in Tehran. They burned U.S. flags, waved placards, and ranted "Death to America. Give us the shah."

Just such a crowd, composed predominantly of women dressed in traditional garb, churned about in Taleghani Street that Sunday morning. By eleven o'clock, the militants had worked themselves into a frenzy. A few young men in the swarm climbed the gate to the compound and opened it from within. As the throng surged into the grounds, the Iranian police stood aside. A U.S. Marine guard raced to the second floor of the chancery building, where Alan Golacinski, the mission's chief of security, was going over some papers. Golacinski rose from his desk to deal with the problem as he had in February, just before the shah fled the country. Then an even more threatening mob had invaded the embassy. Golacinski had stepped out to meet them, and by cool and patient reasoning, he had persuaded them to depart.

But not this time. After some initial progress, Golacinski found a .38-caliber pistol pressed against his temple. The security officer recognized his captors not as student militants at all, but as members of a militia called the Pasadaran.

By then, the compound had filled with rampaging Iranians. They burst into buildings and ransacked rooms, emptying desks and file drawers. In the chancery, the Marines hurried staff members in-

A section of a mural, painted by Iranians on the wall surrounding the U.S. embassy compound in Tehran, depicts events leading to the capture of the embassy. From left to right: The Ayatollah Khomeini returns to Iran from exile in France. As chador-clad women mill about in front of the embassy, Iranian militants scale the compound wall, then parade blindfolded American hostages before the public. A bonfire in the foreground consumes an effigy of President Carter hanging from a gallows.

to a stronghold within the building and donned their flak vests. With great good sense, they did not fire their weapons. It soon became clear that any prolonged resistance would be futile. By midafternoon, all the Americans in the embassy had been taken hostage. Chargé d'Affaires L. Bruce Laingen had been paying a call at the Foreign Ministry when the mob stormed the embassy. He and two Americans accompanying him were detained "for their own safety," as the Iranians put it.

At the Pentagon, an AP teletype machine

installed in the National Military Command Center reported the takeover almost as soon as it occurred. Within minutes, a string of telephone calls originating in the Command Center set in motion a chain of events that would culminate in one of the most audacious rescue operations in military history—a mission whose lessons would be both painful and profound.

One of the telephone calls went to the Delta Force duty officer at Fort Bragg, North Carolina. This unit had been conceived two years earlier for the very purpose of rescuing hostages, especially from hijacked airliners or buildings seized by terrorists. Its commander was a veteran Green Beret colonel named Charlie A. Beckwith. "Chargin' Charlie" was an aggressive and tenacious soldier. In 1966, he had served in Vietnam with a Special Forces unit proficient in long-range reconnaissance deep into Vietcong territory. Grievously wounded, he had recuperated, volunteered again for Vietnam in 1968, then returned stateside to command the Special Forces training school at Fort Bragg. A sign on his desk read: "Kill 'em all. Let God sort 'em out."

eckwith had long been a deeply frustrated man. Years earlier, as a Green Beret captain, he had served a tour in England as part of an exchange program with the British Army's Special Air Service. The SAS was widely regarded as preeminent in the arena of unconventional warfare, and on his return, Beckwith began lobbying for an American unit patterned on it. The Army paid little attention, but Beckwith continued to wage a one-man campaign, updating his proposal from time to time and firing off memos that sometimes impudently skirted the chain of command.

Then, in the early 1970s, a storm of terrorism burst forth. At the Munich Olympics in 1972, Palestinian militants, seeking to focus attention on their cause, murdered eleven Israeli athletes and coaches. The world looked on appalled. Next came a series of terrorist kidnappings, skyjackings, and assaults, many of them barbaric in their bloodshed. European nations of the West responded by training special units to deal with the threats. Britain's SAS turned its skills to antiterrorist tactics; the West Germans set up the formidable Grenzschutzgruppe 9 (GSG-9); the French organized their Groupe d'Intervention de la Gendarmerie Nationale (GIGN).

In 1976, an Israeli strike force scored the first resounding victory against this villainy by rescuing the passengers and crew of an Air France jet hijacked to Entebbe, Uganda. In October of the next year,

West Germany's GSG-9 liberated passengers held inside a Lufthansa airliner at Mogadishu in Somalia. GSG-9 so impressed U.S. president Jimmy Carter that he scribbled a note to General David Jones, the chairman of the Joint Chiefs of Staff: "Do we have the same capability as the West Germans?" After considerable hemming and hawing, the Joint Chiefs conceded that the United States did not.

The order went out for the Army to get going, and almost overnight Charlie Beckwith's oft-rejected plan for an SAS-style unit got on track. Assigned to organize and train the new outfit, Beckwith wanted consummate soldiers—tough, intelligent, highly motivated, and more besides. "We looked for loners. Guys who could operate in the absence of orders," recalled Beckwith. Beyond the usual combat specialties, every volunteer had to contribute some special skill—picking a lock, setting booby-traps, scaling mountains, or hot-wiring a Ford or a Ferrari.

To winnow his Deltas from the merely good soldiers, Beckwith subjected volunteers to harrowing endurance and character tests straight out of the SAS manual. The object, said the colonel, was to measure a man's "real determination, self-discipline, and self-sacrifice." The few who passed this test then underwent

Delta Force commander Colonel Charlie Beckwith was just as tough as he looks in this photograph. Gravely wounded in Vietnam, he arrived at a field hospital so near death that the medical team was ready to give up on him. "Now let's get one thing straight here," he shouted to a startled nurse, "I ain't the average bear, and I didn't come in here to pack it in!" Beckwith survived, and within two years he returned to Vietnam for, as he put it, a "gut check."

a searching interview by Delta Force officers and psychologists. Beckwith wanted men who were willing and able to kill, but not bloodthirsty misfits. To gauge emotional stability, the examiners posed questions that had no correct answers. What would a man do, for example, if he were discovered on a covert mission into enemy territory by two young children? Would he kill the children? Take them with him? Or just disappear? The men were asked about their shortcomings, and if they admitted to none, they were returned to their units.

Beckwith had been given eighteen months to recruit and train an initial Delta Force of 100 men, with an eventual goal of 250. It was a difficult deadline. Of the first 185 volunteers accepted for training, only 53 completed the course. Moreover, the colonel had much work to do refining his recruits' skills at everything from field radio repair to free-fall parachute jumps from 30,000 feet. Delta "operators," as Beckwith termed his shooters to differentiate them from support personnel, became experts with all the exotic paraphernalia of special operations—laser gunsights, night-vision goggles, handguns, and other personal weapons.

Beckwith made his headquarters in a former prison stockade at Bragg. Cells became supply rooms for weapons and equipment. On the stockade grounds were built the props for the core curriculum, including a four-room, $90,000 complex called the Shooting House, where silhouette targets representing both hostages and terrorists popped up at random. In these rooms, Delta shooters learned to make split-second identifications of friend or foe. Training focused on stealth, speed, accurate shooting, and the shock of surprise. Resolve was crucial. A slight hesitation could be disastrous. "There's no more than seven seconds between entering a room and clearing it before things go sour," noted Beckwith. If Delta went into action, no terrorist involved could expect to survive.

In late October 1979, Delta prepared to show its stuff in a certification exercise. The *pièce de résistance* was a simulated hostage rescue at Fort Stewart, Georgia. Examiners invented a scenario as difficult and realistic as they could make it. A group of terrorists, played by other Army personnel, had seized hostages at an airport in a foreign but friendly country. Some were being held in a jetliner, others in a pair of terminal buildings. Simultaneous assaults against both targets would be necessary.

Between the time that Delta Force was alerted until a hostage was "killed," several days passed in mock negotiations with the terrorists. During that interval, the Delta operators worked overtime formulating a plan, and when ordered to execute it, they were under almost as much stress as they could expect during an actual mission. Within seconds, the troops breached all the airliner's entrances and swarmed inside to overpower the terrorists and rescue the hostages. The assault on the terminal buildings, though skillfully executed, started about forty-five seconds after the fireworks began at the airliner, a delay that could cost hostages or Delta shooters their lives. Despite the need for some fine-tuning, the exercise earned Delta Force a rating of C1—fully combat-ready.

The proceedings stretched past midnight on November 4. Afterward, Beckwith retired with his officers to a motel, where they reviewed the exercise and celebrated Delta's graduation. Then the colonel climbed into bed. At 7:00 a.m., the Delta Force duty officer

Thought you ought to know, boss. The American embassy in Tehran has been taken down.

at Fort Bragg awakened him with a phone call. "Thought you ought to know, boss," said the officer. "The American embassy in Tehran has been taken down. The entire staff is being held hostage." Beckwith climbed into his car and drove directly to Fort Bragg, arriving around three o'clock that afternoon to meet with his operators, who had already returned to the stockade. The atmosphere was electric, the squad rooms fairly crackling with anticipation.

Early the following morning, Beckwith received a telephone call from the Pentagon. The Joint Chiefs of Staff wanted a Delta Force representative attached to a special joint task force being set up in Washington to plan a hostage rescue, should the need arise. Major General James Vaught of the U.S. Army, fifty-three years old, assumed command of the task force. Tall, lean, smart, and very determined, Vaught was a Ranger officer who had fought with distinction in Korea and Vietnam. Recently assigned to the Pentagon, this slow-spoken South Carolinian seemed a natural choice—and he faced a daunting challenge.

The hostages were being held halfway around the world, in a remote and intensely hostile city. Beyond news reports, information about the Americans was scant. Before the fundamentalist revolution, the United States had relied chiefly upon the shah's own SAVAK secret police for intelligence, but these were now gone. Guarded by perhaps hundreds of youthful fanatics, the captives might be anywhere within the embassy compound—fourteen buildings spread over twenty-seven acres—or dispersed throughout the city.

Beckwith's troops were eminently capable of storming the embassy or any other building and rescuing the hostages, but this situation presented some unanticipated problems. Delta Force planning assumed that missions would have the cooperation of local governments and armed forces. The unit therefore lacked transportation of its own, the means to ensure its own security while mounting a rescue, and the resources to safeguard liberated hostages. While Beckwith wrestled with the difficulties of sneaking up on the Iranians guarding the embassy, killing them, and freeing the hostages unharmed, Vaught and other officers of the task force had to figure out how to get Delta Force into Iran and out again with the embassy staff.

Beckwith, preferring to be in charge of everything himself, expressed his concern to General Edward Meyer, the Army's chief of

staff and a strong Delta supporter. "Charlie," he said, taking Beckwith aside, "that's really the responsibility of the air people. I don't mind you sticking your nose into it, but it would appear to me that you have a full plate designing the ground tactical plan."

In this as in most military operations, success would depend on keeping the Iranians ignorant of any preparations for a rescue attempt. Surprise had to be complete, and in the months to follow, operational security—OPSEC—would become a vital consideration in everything to do with Operation Rice Bowl, the code name for the rescue mission.

OPSEC, for example, required that Delta Force move quietly out of Fort Bragg. Home to the XVIII Airborne Corps and the famed 82d Airborne Division, historically the Army's quick-reaction force and always in a high state of readiness, Bragg was constantly under the microscopic eye of Soviet intelligence—the target of KGB agents, satellite surveillance, even Aeroflot airliners equipped for electronic snooping as they passed along the North Carolina coast en route to Cuba. Any unusual activity was sure to be noticed. Wearing civilian clothes and traveling hours apart in rented vans and sedans, the Delta operators drove to an isolation site that Beckwith code-named Camp Smokey. Enough support people remained at the stockade to make the headquarters appear as though Delta were still in residence.

To Joint Task Force planners, Beckwith had said: "We need three things—information, information, information." No sooner had Delta arrived at Smokey than technicians installed cryptographic equipment for secure teletype and telephone communications between the camp and the JCS planning team at the Pentagon. The teletype began clattering busily away. However, very little of the material had to do with the location of the hostages or the circumstances of their captivity.

It would take time to collect relevant intelligence, analyze it, and piece it together. Beckwith, as much as those in charge of transportation and logistics for Rice Bowl, needed time to formulate a plan and rehearse it. A similar operation nine years earlier—to rescue American flyers from the Son Tay prison camp outside Hanoi—had taken nearly five months of meticulous preparation, and Tehran was a much tougher nut to crack.

Meanwhile, the State Department was making every possible effort to negotiate the release of the hostages—and arguing against

COMMISSARY

CONSULATE

MARINE GUARD BILLETS

WAREHOUSE

DEPUTY CHIEF OF MISSION'S RESIDENCE

AMBASSADOR'S RESIDENCE

AMJADEIH SOCCER STADIUM

STAFF COTTAGES

MOTOR POOL AREA

CHANCERY

MAIN GATE

This aerial photograph of Tehran shows the arrangement of buildings inside the American embassy compound—as well as the locations of an Iranian military depot and the soccer stadium where Americans taken hostage on November 4, 1979, were to be assembled for evacuation. Delta Force operators planned to scale the compound's east wall *(opposite the soccer stadium)* by ladder. Most of the men would search the buildings for hostages, killing any guards they encountered. The rest would secure the soccer stadium and set up machine-gun positions to protect the hostages as they crossed the street from the embassy compound to the soccer stadium.

even preliminary moves toward military action, afraid of dire consequences for the hostages if the Iranians should learn of such steps. President Carter, however, told the Joint Chiefs to lay the groundwork for a rescue, although he hoped that none would be necessary.

On November 12, General Vaught visited Beckwith at Camp Smokey to settle on one of several possibilities for inserting Delta Force into Iran. Parachuting the shooters into the country was ruled out as too risky; so was sending them in by truck from Turkey. The operation would have to go by helicopter, a solution that also provided a means of evacuating the hostages.

In examining the helicopter option in the days preceding the meeting, planners had settled on the Sikorsky RH-53D Sea Stallion of the U.S. Navy as the helicopter of choice. Powered by twin turboshaft engines driving six-bladed rotors, an RH-53D in a pinch can lift fifty-five troops and their equipment and fly them a distance of 550 nautical miles. Used primarily for minesweeping operations, the Navy aircraft was better suited to the job than a similar Air Force chopper, if only because of the Sea Stallion's folding rotor blades and tail boom. These features permitted cheek-by-jowl storage belowdecks aboard an aircraft carrier, which, because of international relations and OPSEC, seemed to be the only practical launch platform for Delta Force.

Vaught ratified Beckwith's decision that his troops would assault the embassy and spirit away the Americans under cover of darkness. But because a helicopter would take most of a night to reach Tehran, there would be no time left for the actual rescue. So the Delta operators would be ferried to within striking distance of the city the first night and move into Tehran the following evening. During the intervening daylight hours, the assault troops would hide in the mountainous desert, they and their helicopters concealed under camouflage netting. As long as the mission was under cover by daybreak, the Iranians, not expecting visitors, would probably notice nothing.

Upon returning to Washington, Vaught briefed the Joint Chiefs and recommended that six RH-53Ds be assigned to the Joint Task Force and placed aboard the aircraft carrier *Kitty Hawk*, on station in the Indian Ocean. Four helicopters would be needed on the second day to transport the hostages and their rescuers from Tehran to an airfield from which everyone could be extracted by fixed-wing Air Force transports. Two were spares.

Less stern than he appears in this official army portrait, General James Vaught was already a much-decorated paratrooper and Ranger officer when he was assigned the job of extricating American hostages from Iran. Earlier in his career, Vaught had served combat tours in both Korea and Vietnam before taking charge of the 24th Infantry Division in 1977. In his role as commander of the rescue task force, Vaught was a methodical planner who insisted that his staff constantly review evolving mission plans for weaknesses—and correct them.

The particular machines—from a fleet of thirty built in the mid-1970s—belonged to East Coast chopper units based near Norfolk, Virginia. With some disassembly, two of the 30,000-pound helicopters were loaded into the vast cargo hold of an Air Force C-5A Galaxy. They were taken to the British island of Diego Garcia in the Indian Ocean, then flown surreptitiously to the *Kitty Hawk*. Maintenance crews on the carrier would remove minesweeping gear and install auxiliary fuel tanks that added 200 nautical miles to the helicopters' range. The crews would also fit the choppers with sophisticated Omega and PINS navigation systems. Omega is a very low frequency radio system capable of giving a pilot his location within a few miles anywhere in the world. PINS (Palletized Inertial Navigation System), supplied with a helicopter's starting point, can keep track of the aircraft's position within a few hundred yards.

Although the Sea Stallion could take on fuel in flight from KC-130 tankers, doing so was impractical. Launched from Diego Garcia—the only base within 2,000 nautical miles of Iran that the planners could count on using—the tankers would have a round trip that exceeded their range substantially, and the KC-130 was not equipped for tanking up in flight. However, the capability for taking on fuel in flight was built into other models of the C-130; they could be used to carry fuel to a rendezvous with the helicopters in the bleak Iranian desert. Upon landing, the choppers would be gassed up with enough fuel to carry the Delta operators to the hide site and the next night to airlift the liberated hostages from the embassy to the airfield for the flight out of Iran. Thus, for the operation to succeed, three sites would be needed in Iran: a place to refuel on the way in, a place to hide, and an airfield from which to evacuate the hostages.

Task-force planners soon found a field for the airlift out of Iran—Manzariyeh, thirty minutes south of Tehran by helicopter. There, in the glory days of the shah, the Iranian Air Force had maintained a bombing range, complete with a paved 10,000-foot runway. On the second night of Rice Bowl, a force of seventy-five U.S. Army Rangers, transported by C-130 to Manzariyeh, would seize the facility and hold it while a pair of Lockheed C-141 Starlifters—big, four-engine jet transports second in size only to the Galaxies—rumbled in to evacuate everyone.

A second, larger meeting convened at Camp Smokey on December 2. This time General Vaught brought with him most of his staff, including Air Force Colonel James Kyle, a former air commando, who had joined the team as its air officer; he knew his business and impressed the Delta operators. The meeting was to complete the plan for inserting Delta Force and recovering them, along with the hostages, from Iran. After six hours of detailed discussion, the pieces were falling into place. A task-force planner turned to Charlie Beckwith and asked: "Colonel, how many of your men will be required to handle the mission?" Beckwith answered that he needed seventy. "Goddammit, Charlie, that's too many," said Vaught. But Beckwith stuck to his assessment, arguing that he would need at least that many operators to assault a compound the size of a small college campus, seize and search more than a dozen buildings, cover the major avenue running past the compound, and shepherd terrified hostages onto the helicopters. Seventy shooters it would be—Beckwith's entire force at the time, although another group of operators had reached an advanced stage of training.

As Christmas approached, Beckwith ordered his men home to Fort Bragg. They would spend the holidays there as they usually did, in order to preserve the deception that Delta Force was doing nothing out of the ordinary.

At the stockade, the work continued. Raw intelligence had to be analyzed, slowly and painstakingly. Delta shooters had to adjust their weapons and tactics. They had trained to pick out terrorists from hostages in confined quarters with the faithful Colt .45-caliber automatic pistol, "accurized," as Beckwith put it, by Delta's own gunsmiths. These experts replaced loose-fitting parts typical of the mass-produced weapon with custom-built pieces having closer tolerances. They added target-pistol trigger mechanisms and better sights. Yet for Iran, where Delta Force expected more opposition than a few airplane hijackers could offer, the .45 pistol became a side arm. The room-clearing weapon for this mission would be the M3A1 Colt .45-caliber submachine gun, also accurized.

Some firearms experts fault the 1911-vintage .45-caliber round for its low muzzle velocity—about 850 feet per second compared with 1,200 feet per second for handguns of more recent design, so slow, said Beckwith, that "standing behind it you can actually see the slug moving." He exaggerated to make a point. In a confined space, such as an airplane cabin, the heavy, 230-grain bullet "will knock a man slap down, but may not exit the target," according to Beckwith. A higher-powered bullet, he advised, "will likely go through a terrorist, through a seat, and end up in an innocent bystander."

To seal off streets near the embassy against any countering reaction by Iranian troops, 7.62-mm M-60 machine guns were to be carried along. Some of the operators also trained with 40-mm grenade launchers accurate to 400 yards and polished their skills with the C-4 plastic high explosive necessary to blast through heavy doors and brick walls.

To help Beckwith plan his assault on the embassy, an eight-foot-by-twelve-foot model of the compound and the surrounding streets had been built. Roofs and floors of the buildings could be removed like layers of a cake, permitting close study of rooms and corridors from top floor to basement. In the evenings, the Delta intelligence team watched the television news coverage of Iran. It showed how the gates were secured (a padlock on the motor pool, for example), what weapons the guards carried (a motley assortment), whether they had grenades (none were observed), and whether they handled themselves like professionals (more like amateurs, it was agreed). The team took careful note of the traffic in the streets outside and carefully assessed where the machine guns might be best deployed.

o far, however, no one had discovered precisely where the Iranians were holding the hostages. And there was another elusive piece of information the Delta planners hoped to uncover: the location in Tehran of the Iranians' armored vehicles and other heavy weaponry. Some 23-mm antiaircraft cannon were particularly worrisome. Their twin barrels could be depressed to fire at targets on the ground, and lightly armed Delta rescuers would be vulnerable to such firepower.

Nevertheless, recalled Beckwith, the Delta planners "began to color in the black-and-white sketch they carried in their mind's eye." Tactics and timing were critical. Every move had to be perfectly coordinated if the operators were not to injure one another. "This thing has got to be like a ballet," coached an assault-element leader one day while rehearsing his men in room clearing. "We've got to have this choreographed just right, got to know what steps you're taking and those of your buddy. We've got to do this in concert." Shortly afterward, someone posted a cartoon of Delta's shooters, dressed in ballerinas' tutus, pirouetting into the embassy with their burp guns.

To complicate matters, Chargé d'Affaires Laingen and the two other Americans being held at the Foreign Ministry would also have to be rescued. In the hands of the Iranian government, they had at first been allowed visitors and seemed relatively safe compared with the hostages at the embassy, whom the Iranians regularly threatened with execution. But after a few weeks, the Americans at the Foreign Ministry were isolated under lock and key. They seemed little better off than their compatriots sixteen blocks away.

About this time, Vaught and Beckwith had their first look at the aircrews assigned to fly the Sea Stallions. Initially, the pilots were a mix of Navy officers who were intimately familiar with the RH-53D and Marines trained to fly combat assault missions in a variant of the aircraft. Neither group had much experience flying long distances at night, and the Navy pilots flew precisely by the book—as they would on a minesweeping mission. "We wanted aces," recalled Beckwith. "Daredevils, barnstormers, hot rodders, guys who could pick it up, turn it around on a dime, and put it back down with a flair."

In mid-December, the helicopter pilots moved to a training base in the West, where they could practice formation flying at night in desert conditions, whirling along with their running lights extinguished to simulate flying across Iran. The pilots wore PVS-5 night-vision goggles that made it possible to see the horizon, the ground, and the rest of the formation in the dead of night. But the goggles gave only twenty-seventy acuity, no depth perception, and only half the normal field of vision. An aviator wearing them could be considered legally blind. Eyestrain caused by the goggles brought on splitting headaches after thirty minutes, and pilots had to trade off with their copilots.

The Navy pilots struggled, and by Christmas all but one would be replaced. Substituting Air Force pilots practiced at flying long distances in a helicopter similar to the Sea Stallion was considered but proved to be impractical. Doing so would have required transition training into the Navy version of the aircraft, adding time to a tight, though undefined, schedule. Moreover, no single Air Force unit had enough such pilots to supply Operation Rice Bowl. Bringing them together from the four corners of the globe would have resulted in a chopper element no more accustomed to working together than were the Navy and Marine flyers. In the event, the Marines gathered additional pilots from as far away as Okinawa, and the men trained intensively to bring their long-distance, nighttime flying skills up to snuff. Before long, the Marines were making heartening progress under Lieutenant Colonel Edward Seiffert, a first-rate aviator who got along well with both Kyle and Beckwith.

Flying a helicopter compares with piloting a fixed-wing aircraft as riding a unicycle compares with pedaling a bicycle. Control surfaces of a C-130, for example, can be adjusted so that it flies straight and level without constant attention from the pilot. However, a helicopter—particularly one that is flying at low altitude—can fall out of the sky if the pilot's attention strays. Even with a copilot to share the load, flying hour after hour under such strain is no job for the inexperienced. The Marines knew they had a lot of work ahead before they mastered the mission's intensely difficult and dangerous flight regime. After weeks of practice, their first test came on December 21—a 600-mile, six-and-a-half-hour night flight using the PVS-5 goggles. The object was to stay on course and on time, and the Marines succeeded.

The PVS-5 night-vision goggles worn by Marine pilots flying helicopters to Desert One have dual lenses that can be focused individually and tilted to align with the eyes of the wearer. Superseded by newer models in the late 1980s, PVS-5s were powered by a special three-volt lithium battery about half the length of a flashlight battery and good for one night's operation.

Amid rescue preparations, the quality of intelligence about the hostages had begun to improve. In mid-November, the Iranians had released thirteen of the sixty-six hostages. From interviews with the freed Americans, analysts learned that the remaining captives had been divided into small groups and locked in several buildings within the embassy compound. Furthermore, the CIA managed to reinfiltrate one of its Iranian agents, code-named Franco, into Tehran. Franco had left Iran shortly after the shah. His control was a CIA officer code-named Bob who, posing as a European businessman, would be able to pass in and out of Iran.

Task-force intelligence analysts began to identify some of the buildings where the hostages were being held. After a time, all but four of the fourteen structures were ruled out, and Delta operators began to frame a detailed, room-by-room assault plan. Among the buildings was the chancery, a difficult target. It was a long, three-story affair—a "hardened" structure, built of brick and having either security bars or shutters on the windows.

Another issue resolved itself after Bob and Franco arrived on the scene. The task force had been puzzling about how the Delta shooters would move from the hide site to the embassy on the second night. Choppers flying low over the city would rouse all of Tehran, so Bob received instructions to buy six two-and-a-half-ton trucks—plus a couple of vans—for the purpose and to stash them in a warehouse on the outskirts of town until the night of the operation.

By this time, the Delta contingent had grown to ninety-two operators and had broken its two squadrons into Red, Blue, and White elements. Red and Blue were to clear the embassy grounds, search the target buildings room by room, and free the hostages. White was to support the assault teams and secure the streets outside the compound. Beckwith loaded them all on C-130s and flew west to practice with the helicopters. While there, he observed the first field tests of a system that everybody hoped would solve the refueling problem for the RH-53Ds. It was a bust.

The idea was to parachute huge rubber fuel cells called blivets onto the desert where the helicopters could land and fill their tanks. A blivet resembled a pair of huge inner tubes joined by an axle. Designed to be rolled along the ground by several men, each blivet held 500 gallons of JP-4 jet fuel. On the first run, the blivets came hurtling out of a low-flying C-130—and burst open on the ground in great cascading blossoms of fuel. The parachutes had failed to open. Eventually, the parachute riggers got it right, and the blivets landed softly. But weighing more than 1,200 pounds, they proved extremely difficult to manhandle on the ground. Moreover, pumping the JP-4 into the helicopters simply took too long. The Joint Task Force would have to find another way.

Meanwhile, Delta Force's estimated manpower needs continued to grow. Beckwith now felt he needed 120 men, including support personnel. It had become increasingly clear that the six Sea Stallions originally ordered would be enough for the job only if none of them broke. Revised plans called for all six to be flyable at the refueling spot. Otherwise, the mission would have to be scrubbed. One consideration was that the helicopter engines would be shut down during the day at the hide site and restarted for the flight into Tehran that night. Aboard a carrier, there was electrical power to crank the engines as long as necessary

An empty fuel bladder lies in a C-130 at Florida's Hurlburt Field, where the aircraft were prepared for helicopter-refueling rehearsals in the Arizona desert. A valve assembly, called a top, routes fuel through hoses to dual pump and filter units at the plane's rear. The hose in the foreground is used to fill the bladders from a fuel tank. At Desert One, hoses stowed between the filter units were stretched to the choppers.

to fire them up, but in the field, each Sea Stallion would have two compressed-air tanks to get started. An engine that failed to catch before the air ran out would render one of the big birds useless. With such facts in mind, task-force planners added two more RH-53Ds to the force. Experience in Vietnam, however, had shown the machines to be so unreliable that, for every two undertaking a mission, one backup was needed. That arithmetic argued for an additional helicopter. But no more would fit aboard the carrier *Nimitz*, which had replaced the *Kitty Hawk* on station in the Indian Ocean, without removing some of the *Nimitz*'s normal complement of aircraft and, in the view of the Navy, unacceptably diminishing the carrier's operational capabilities.

Success of the mission depended on clear skies. Early on, planners had decided that foul weather would be a potentially fatal complication of an already complex undertaking. Air Force meteorologists made forecast after forecast over a period of months, comparing their assessments against the actual weather in Iran until they became reasonably sure of their skill in predicting large patterns of inclement weather. However, foreseeing local weather systems proved impossible. The route into Iran was purposely remote. A weather satellite covered the area, but Iran published no ground or airways reports, the kind of information necessary to make accurate local forecasts. Thus, the meteorologists had no hope of predicting a particularly hazardous phenomenon called a haboob—a cloud of suspended dust stirred up by a thunderstorm.

Since the helicopters were to keep each other in sight during the flight and navigate by picking out landmarks on the ground, a haboob could spell serious trouble. However, the haboob season was waning, and like thunderstorms, the dust clouds rarely formed at night. Information uncovered about haboobs appeared in the weather annex to the Rice Bowl plan.

Task-force planners meanwhile had figured out where Delta would lay up for the day—in a wadi, a dry riverbed, near an improved road fifty miles southeast of Tehran. The Sea Stallions would be concealed in a more rugged area fifteen miles away. There they would wait until they were summoned by radio into Tehran. The main pickup point would be the Amjadeih soccer stadium across the street from the embassy compound. Delta could easily seal off the high-walled stadium, and the helicopters could land, load, and depart for the airstrip at Manzariyeh more or less protected from small-arms fire.

One major element of the plan had yet to be pinned down—where and how to refuel in the desert. Even before the disappointing performance by the blivets, the search had been on for a place to land C-130s carrying JP-4 for the choppers, doing away with the cumbersome fuel bladders. Higher-capacity pumps on board the planes would speed the transfer of fuel. By late December, intelligence analysts had isolated a likely candidate in the vast Dasht-e-Kavir salt desert, some 250 nautical miles southeast of Tehran. A dirt road bisected the site, but it appeared to be lightly traveled. No one could be certain that the ground would support the 120,000-pound weight of a fuel-laden C-130. Someone had to go in and find out.

Vaught attempted to sell the idea of a reconnaissance mission to the Joint Chiefs and then to the White House. A month passed. Then, in mid-February, the request was denied; the prospects for a negotiated hostage release looked a bit more promising.

By now Delta Force was "leaning forward," as Charlie Beckwith put it. Everybody wanted to go. Winter cold embraced Tehran, and the embassy guards could be seen huddled around fires built in empty oil drums. They would not be overly alert.

General Vaught personally observed the seventh dry run in the Arizona desert in late March. Delta operators rehearsed every aspect of the Tehran assault. As Beckwith wrote later: "The truck ride was made, role-playing guards were taken out as they patrolled a mock compound wall, the wall was climbed, dummy buildings were hit and cleared, the chopper rendezvous was made, the Rangers—at a make-believe Manzariyeh—seized the airstrip and held it while the C-141s lifted everyone out. Seventh time, and it had gone as smoothly as the *X*s and *O*s on the blackboard.''

While out West, Beckwith learned that the soil-sampling mission to the proposed refueling point had at last been approved. On the night of March 30, flying a light, twin-engine aircraft, a pair of CIA pilots landed an Air Force combat controller near the dirt road at the Dasht-e-Kavir site. Under a thick layer of dust, the ground seemed solid. The Air Force officer inserted the probe of an instrument called a penetrometer into the soil to gauge the density; it would support the C-130 tankers. He also took core samples for laboratory analysis to determine the effect of water on the soil and how long after a rain it would take to dry. Mounting a motorbike that he had unloaded from the plane, he next laid out two airstrips flanking the road and marked each with six radio-activated infrared lights. The pair of airstrips would divide the C-130s and helicopters into two groups, reducing congestion at the temporary airfield. The controller was on the ground for ninety minutes, and during that time several vehicles had passed. He clearly saw the face of one driver as the Iranian lit a cigarette, but, gaze locked on his headlight beams, the man at the wheel looked neither left nor right and did not see the American on the motorbike or the aircraft parked a short distance away. Within two days, the wind had blown away the furrows left in the sand by the aircraft's landing gear. It was as if no one had been there.

Plans had originally called for the assault forces to fly off the aircraft carrier in the helicopters. But the newfound refueling spot, named Desert One, suggested a better course. Delta assault teams would go to Desert One aboard C-130s and transfer there to the refueled helicopters. Flying empty the 500 miles or so from the Gulf of Oman to Desert One would require less fuel.

But now six C-130s would be required. In addition to JP-4 for eight helicopters, they had to carry a force of 130 or so—Beckwith and his Delta operators, a Green Beret team to assault the Foreign Ministry, a road-watch team of Rangers to secure Desert One, drivers for the trucks, and Kyle's combat control team. Finally, a pair of former Iranian generals was added to the roster. Their job would be to break in on the Iranian military radio network if necessary and create chaos by issuing false orders.

When the force arrived at Desert One, Colonel Kyle would be in charge until the helicopters took off for the hide site. After that, Beckwith would take over. General Vaught would remain at a command post outside Iran.

Plans had also been developed to rescue the three men at the Foreign Ministry. Since the Delta shooters already had their hands full with the embassy assault, a thirteen-man team of Green Berets from the 10th Special Forces Group in West Germany would join Rice Bowl. Two Green Beret sergeants had been infiltrated into Iran to case the lightly guarded Foreign Ministry. They then returned to Germany and proposed a scheme that relied on stealth. Two of the team would scale the walls to the window of the third-floor office known to hold the hostages. Detection was unlikely, but if the guards in the corridor heard something and entered the room, they would be killed. The pair of Green Berets would help the three hostages to the ground and guide them to a nearby open area where a helicopter would pick them up.

There was still the question of the 23-mm antiaircraft cannon; they had not been seen. As a counter, Vaught and the task-force planners decided to add a couple of AC-130 Spectre gunships to the mission *(pages 145-147)*. These aircraft carry stunning firepower, ranging from 20-mm Gatling guns and 40-mm Bofors pompoms to a heavy 105-mm howitzer that could knock out any Iranian armored vehicles. One AC-130 would orbit the embassy and the soccer stadium, while the other would cover Tehran's Mehrabad International Airport, where a pair of Iranian Air Force F-4 Phantoms were known to be on strip alert. Should the fighters move to take off, they would be destroyed as they taxied to the runway.

At 6:30 on the evening of April 16, Beckwith, Kyle, Vaught, and General David Jones briefed President Carter at the White House. Vaught went over the mission step by step: how Delta Force would fly to Desert One and rendezvous with the Sea Stallions; how it would then helicopter to its daytime hide site; how the next evening after sunset it would convoy into Tehran; how a four-man Delta team would shoot the embassy sentries with silenced pistols; how Delta operators would scale the wall.

Once inside the compound, Blue and Red elements, forty men each, would assault and clear the buildings, shooting the guards and

Metamorphosis of a Cargo Plane

Cannon blasting, an AC-130H Spectre gunship circles its target as if tethered to it by a chain of deadly projectiles. As long as the pilot keeps the wing tip pointed at the target, the guns can fire round after round at the spot without changing aim—except to compensate for sideways drift of the aircraft caused by cross winds.

In the early 1960s, United States Air Force technicians at Bienhoa Air Base in Vietnam installed three six-barrel 7.62-mm Gatling-style Miniguns pointing through the door and left-side windows of a World War II-vintage C-47 transport. Named the AC-47 (*A* stands for attack), this aircraft and others like it saved the lives of many an American soldier. In night attacks, Spooky—the AC-47's radio call sign—time and again directed a devastating fire against enemy troops poised to overrun a friendly outpost.

So effective was the AC-47 that the Air Force made a better Spooky from a much larger transport—the C-130. Equipped with night-vision devices and armed with more and bigger guns than its predecessor, the AC-130 Spectre gunship became a hunter, patrolling the lightly defended Ho Chi Minh Trail by night in an effort to disrupt the flow of enemy supplies through Laos. During the next two decades or so, the AC-130 evolved into a potent and accurate weapons system.

A Spectre gunship carries a flight crew of six, plus eight people to operate sensors and weapons. Five gunners labor in the dim fuselage to keep the guns loaded and ready; a fire-control officer (FCO) and two sensor operators scan the ground for targets with infrared sensors and low-light-level television. Even on a pitch-dark night, the pictures are nearly indistinguishable from ordinary black-and-white television—except for the cross hairs etched on the screens. A computer assists in aiming the guns so accurately that at a range of 5,000 feet projectiles will strike within five feet of the aiming point. With the target identified, the FCO alerts sensor operators, gunners, and pilot, who gives permission to fire. When all is ready, the sensor operator releases the last in a series of safety mechanisms, and firing commences.

ABRISTLE WITH SENSORS AND WEAPONS

All of the AC-130H Spectre's target-detection gear and armament is arrayed on the left side of the aircraft. Below the cockpit is a radio direction finder that can home in on a radio beacon when aiding troops under fire, or on the electronic noise produced by enemy vehicles' ignition systems. At a door just aft of the nose wheel is a sensor mount that supports a low-light-level television camera (LLLTV), which uses a photomultiplier to amplify even faint traces of starlight, and a laser for finding the range to a target or marking targets for laser-guided bombs, usually dropped by jet fighter-bombers. Installed in a wheel well is an infrared sensor that displays an image created from the heat a target emits. A powerful searchlight can also be used to illuminate targets for the LLLTV.

Armament consists of two six-barrel 20-mm Vulcan cannon ahead of the wing for use against troops and light vehicles. A 40-mm Bofors automatic cannon, intended for trucks and light armor, is aft of the main landing gear. Sparkle rounds can be fired from the Bofors to mark targets for night fighter attack. Beacon-tracking radar, protected behind a bubble next to the Bofors, uses radar beacons sent out by friendly forces as reference points for aiming the guns. Farthest aft is a 105-mm howitzer; its thirty-two-pound projectile can destroy tanks and buildings.

RADIO DIRECTION FINDER

LOW-LIGHT-LEVEL TELEVISION AND LASER

20-MM VULCAN CANNON

INFRARED SENSOR

ELECTRONIC COUNTERMEASURE POD

A brace of 20-mm Vulcan automatic cannon poke from their gunports. Firing 40 high-explosive rounds per second, the Vulcan emits a low moan rather than the staccato report of much slower-firing machine guns.

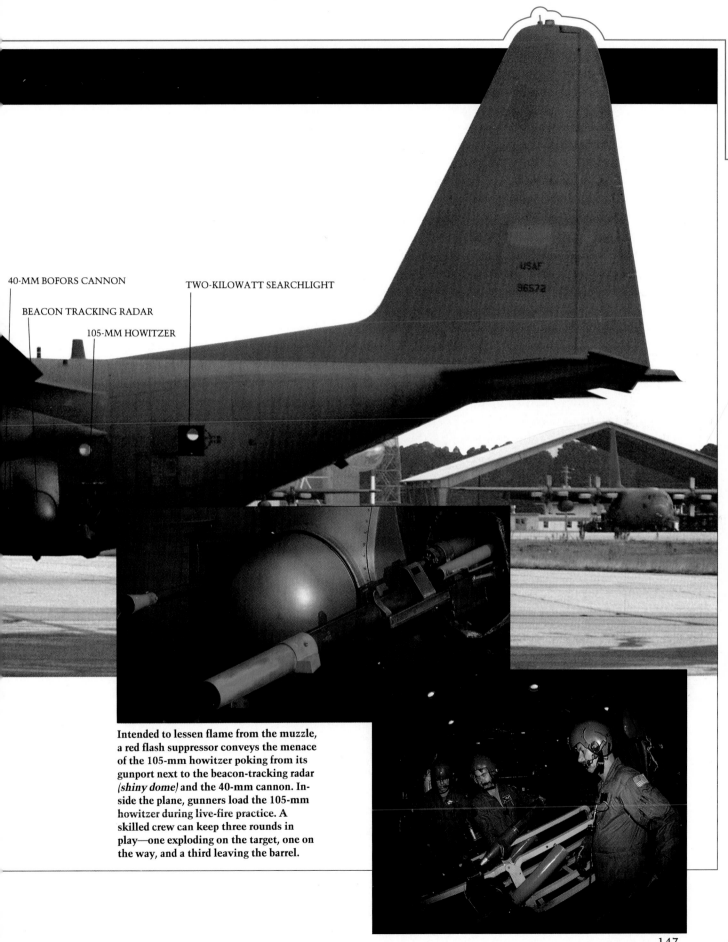

40-MM BOFORS CANNON

BEACON TRACKING RADAR

105-MM HOWITZER

TWO-KILOWATT SEARCHLIGHT

USAF
96572

Intended to lessen flame from the muzzle, a red flash suppressor conveys the menace of the 105-mm howitzer poking from its gunport next to the beacon-tracking radar *(shiny dome)* and the 40-mm cannon. Inside the plane, gunners load the 105-mm howitzer during live-fire practice. A skilled crew can keep three rounds in play—one exploding on the target, one on the way, and a third leaving the barrel.

freeing the hostages. Meanwhile, the smaller White element would control the streets and seize the stadium. Covered by White's three machine guns, Blue and Red would hustle the hostages through a hole blown in the compound wall and across the street to the stadium where the Sea Stallions would swoop down and pick them up.

The president asked about possible casualties. Vaught said that six or seven Deltas might be hit, along with two or three hostages. Deputy Secretary of State Warren Christopher wanted to know about the guards; would Delta just neutralize them, shoot them in the shoulder or something? "No sir," replied Beckwith. He went on to explain that he expected to find no more than twenty-five guards on duty in the hallways. They would all be killed.

Finally, President Carter said: "It's time for me to summarize. I do not want to undertake this mission, but we have no recourse. The only way I will call it off now is for the International Red Cross to hand our Americans back. We are going to do this mission." The date was set for April 24, little more than a week away.

Since mid-November, JTF planners had been looking for an alternative to flying Delta Force from the United States directly to Diego Garcia. They also hoped to find a departure point for the C-130s close enough to Iran that the aircraft could complete the mission on one tank of fuel. Since the so-called Camp David Accords between Israel, Egypt, and the United States in 1978, American military advisers had been training Egyptian Army, Air Force, and Navy and, from time to time, conducting joint exercises. Relatively close to Iran, Egypt would be a convenient stopover point and command-post location. However, OPSEC considerations dictated that Anwar Sadat, Egypt's president, could not be approached until just before the mission. In early December, the U.S. European Command had stepped up the number of flights into Egypt to mask the assembly there of Rice Bowl forces should that course of action be approved. When presented with the plan, Sadat agreed.

From Egypt, the distance to Iran was still greater than the unrefueled range of the C-130s. With five days to go, U.S. diplomats sought and received permission from the sultan of Oman to launch the C-130s carrying Delta Force and the helicopter fuel from Masirah Island. Use of the island, situated in the Indian Ocean much closer to Iran than Egypt, simplified Rice Bowl significantly. Now the C-130s could make it to Desert One and back without refueling, although as a precaution, tankers would be on call.

For all the good work by Bob, the CIA agent in Tehran, the Joint Task Force and Charlie Beckwith felt uneasy about arrangements for the trucks and the hide site. For months, Beckwith had wanted a man of his own on the scene. Richard Meadows volunteered to go. Since his role in the raid on Son Tay prison camp *(Chapter 2)*, he had retired from the Army and become a civilian adviser to Delta Force.

On April 21, Meadows entered Tehran. Posing as a European businessman, he smuggled in a special radio to communicate with Washington by satellite. With him went a young Iranian-born Air Force sergeant code-named Fred. In addition, the two Green Beret sergeants who had reconnoitered the Foreign Ministry reentered Tehran. Using a house rented by Franco as a base, the reception team made their final preparations. Fred inspected the six British Ford trucks and the two vans that Bob had purchased. Meadows drove into the foothills to see the hide site where Delta would spend the day. It lay too close to a railway line, so he chose another not far away. He covered the route to the embassy, walked around the compound, studied the guards from a café across the way, and had a look at the soccer stadium. Satisfied, he sent an innocuous cable to a contact in England, inserting the phrase "piece of cake."

By then Delta had moved to Egypt, where they camped out in a concrete hangar at an abandoned Soviet-built MiG base at Wadi Qena, 300 miles south of Cairo. Two command shelters for General Vaught, equipped with satellite communications gear, had been flown in a few days earlier and positioned nearby. That night, Vaught and Beckwith received an interesting bit of information: The Iranians had released the embassy cook and his wife, both Middle Easterners. On the flight out of Iran, they had by pure chance been seated next to the CIA's Franco, who was leaving as well. Franco immediately recognized the prize and arranged for them to be debriefed when the plane landed in Frankfurt, West Germany. However, the interview was disappointing. The cook and his wife had not been in contact with the hostages and could only guess where the Americans were being held.

For thirty-six hours, the force rested at Wadi Qena. Beckwith's men spent the time cleaning their weapons and adjusting their body clocks to Middle Eastern time. At 6:00 a.m. on April 24, the colonel inspected his operators, all of them dressed in jeans, flak vests,

149

black field jackets, unshined combat boots, and navy blue watch caps. One of the officers read a passage from 1 Samuel about David and Goliath—and then the men spontaneously broke into a roaring "God Bless America." Three hours later, 132 men filed on board C-141 Starlifters bound for Masirah Island. There, the troops would transfer to the C-130s for the flight to Desert One and the rendezvous with the choppers.

Aboard the USS *Nimitz* steaming sixty miles from the Iranian coast, Lieutenant Colonel Edward Seiffert, call sign Dash 1, lifted his Sea Stallion off the flight deck at dusk. Within minutes, his RH-53D and the other seven formed a loose diamond formation and together set off northward at 120 knots. All were painted desert tan without insignia. Now, in the fading light, the pilots adjusted their PVS-5 goggles for the flight to Desert One, 540 nautical miles away. The goggles, though a continuing discomfort, were, as Seiffert said, "better than having no eyes at all."

The choppers proceeded under strict radio silence. If something

Yellow-jerseyed aircraft handlers go about the task of moving the helicopters into position for takeoff from the flight deck of the *Nimitz*. The red-jerseyed sailor driving a squat vehicle called a tug is responsible for loading munitions onto aircraft in preparation for a mission.

went wrong, the crew of one helicopter could inform the others by means of simple, prearranged light signals. Pilots would eyeball their way from one checkpoint to the next, using the Omega and PINS systems as a cross-check on position if necessary. They crossed the Iranian coast at an altitude of 100 feet, midway between two Iranian radar stations. Then, flying 200 feet above the ground, the helicopters followed the rising terrain through a mountain pass at 4,600 feet. "Once we crossed that first mountain, all the checkpoints kept coming up," said Major James Schaefer in Dash 3. "It was very reassuring."

One of the chopper pilots had seen the lead C-130 passing close overhead. The plane carried Beckwith, the forty Deltas of Major Logan Fitch's Blue element, the road-watch team of Army Rangers, the combat control team to manage traffic at Desert One, the mission truck drivers, and Colonel Kyle, the air boss—eighty-eight passengers in all, plus LAW (light antitank weapon) rockets and Redeye heat-seeking antiaircraft missiles, two off-road motorcycles, and a Jeep. Just getting off the ground had been a feat. And if the heavily laden craft lost an engine during the first hour of flight—"Well," said the pilot, Lieutenant Colonel Bob Brenci, "that'll be kiss-off time."

Four hours later, within twenty miles of Desert One, Brenci toggled a radio transmitter to activate the infrared landing-strip lights set out three and a half weeks earlier. Brenci's plane and two others following were MC-130s, also known as Combat Talon aircraft. Specifically outfitted for special operations, each was equipped with forward-looking infrared (FLIR), a television-like camera that produces an image from heat rather than visible light. As Brenci approached to land, the FLIR revealed a truck on the nearby road. He immediately pulled up and around to let the vehicle clear. Then he put the plane down—hard—at 10:40 p.m. It was the "worst landing of my life," he recalled later. Kyle radioed Vaught at Wadi Qena: "Foreman, Woodpecker. Q Tip." No Iranian would intercept the signal, which was beamed upward to a communications satellite overhead.

Delta had arrived, but already the operation had slipped ten minutes behind schedule. Time was critical. Delta had to reach the hide site before first light, and on that night there would be only nine hours, sixteen minutes of darkness. Refueling included, the trip was planned for eight hours.

The men filed out of the C-130, and the Rangers set off to block the road. They were not yet in position when a pair of headlights approached. As the lights drew closer, a Ranger opened up with an M-16 on automatic. A large bus shuddered to a stop, the engine riddled. A Ranger sergeant leaped on board and stood in the aisle covering forty-three terrified Iranians with his assault rifle. Rice Bowl planners had prepared for this. Prisoners would be flown out on the C-130s and returned the next night to Manzariyeh on the C-141s scheduled to evacuate the hostages.

Almost immediately, another set of headlights gleamed through the dust. Someone tried to flag down the vehicle. It kept coming, so a Ranger loosed a shoulder-fired LAW rocket. The vehicle, a fuel truck, exploded in flames 300 feet high. More lights. A pickup truck slewed to a halt. Jumping from his cab, the driver of the burning vehicle raced to the pickup, which spun around and sped off. A Ranger jumped on his dirt bike to give chase, but the motor refused to start until the pickup was fast disappearing.

Probably smugglers, thought Beckwith, and not likely to rush to the police. Besides, the colonel had other things on his mind. Dick Meadows in Tehran had just radioed, using a very short burst transmission difficult for an enemy to catch: "All the groceries are on the shelf." He was ready with the trucks.

The other five C-130s arrived on schedule, but the helicopters had run into difficulty. Two hours away from the *Nimitz*, a warning light flashed on the instrument panel of Dash 6. A sensor had noted a drop in the pressure of nitrogen gas sealed inside the hollow spar of the chopper's rotor blades to alert pilots to the possibility of a crack. Dash 6 landed immediately, accompanied by Dash 8. Another indicator on the rotor hub confirmed the loss of pressure. Lightly loaded and flying slowly, the helicopter might have withstood several hours' use. But the aircraft would be heavy taking off from Desert One and would have to travel at nearly top speed—too risky. Dash 6 would fly no farther. Collecting classified documents and personal gear, the crew abandoned their machine and piled into Dash 8.

At the three-hour mark, the chopper pilots encountered a great white wall of dust—a freak haboob. The talc-fine powder swallowed up the aircraft. Visibility plummeted to less than a hundred feet. "It was like flying into a bowl of milk," one pilot recalled. Ed Seiffert turned Dash 1 around and, with his wing man close behind,

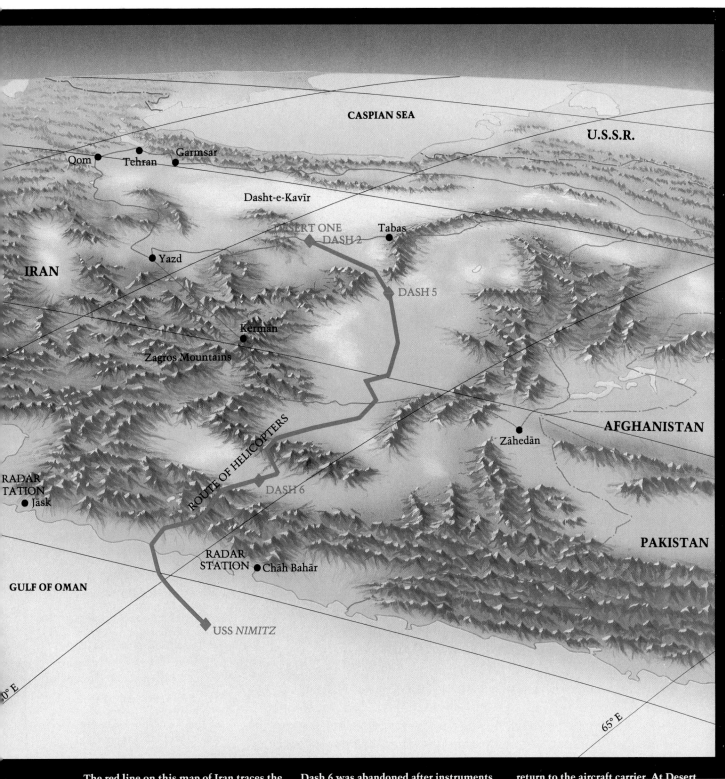

The red line on this map of Iran traces the helicopter route from the *Nimitz* to Desert One. Crossing the Iranian coastline at low altitudes midway between two radar stations, the choppers headed through a mountain pass. Soon after, helicopter Dash 6 was abandoned after instruments warned of a faulty rotor blade. After more mountains, the remaining choppers encountered haboobs, or dense clouds of suspended dust; Dash 5 developed instrument problems and forced the pilot to return to the aircraft carrier. At Desert One, Dash 2 was declared unairworthy because of hydraulic failure. Plans to proceed to the hide site near Garmsar were then canceled, and the rescue attempt was called off.

ROUTE	DESC	CAS	DIST	A/S	TIME	ELAPSE	COORDINATES
SHIP			0	—	(1805)	—	N 25° 23.5 E 59° 39.0
CIP	ROAD X RIVER		50	120	27 (1832)	29	N 25 43.0 E 59 33.0
TP#1	STREAM BED	345	19	120	10 (1844)	39	N 26° 35.3 E 59° 56.8
TP#2	STREAM BED IN SMOKE	326	63	120	32 (1916)	1+11	N 29° 33.7 E 59 43.0
TP#3	ROAD X RIVER	354	119	130	55 (2011)	2+06	N 29 33 E 59 58.6
TP#4	CORNER DRY LAKE	021	61	130	28 (2039)	2+33	N 33° 04.3 E 55 53.0
REFUEL	SIDE OF ROAD	321	65	140	11 (2050)	(4+28)	
GROUND TIME		—	—	—	(6589)		N 33 04.6 E 58 45.7
TP#5	ROAD INTX	269	06	80	5 (2050)	5	
TP#6	ROAD INTX (ELEV 2530)	302	208	105	119 (2201)	2+04	N 35 33.7 E 52 20.7
TP#7	RAILROAD TRACKS	309	10.5	100	7 (2208)	2+11	N 35 11.0 E 52 10.6
0Z		028	3	100	2 (2210)	2+13	N 35 13.4 E 52 12.6
GROUND TIME LAAGER		20?	?	100	5 (2311)	2+18	N 35 13.3 E 52 13.3

flew out of the dust cloud and landed. Since the operational plan called for at least five miles' visibility, the haboob constituted grounds for aborting the mission. Seiffert's radio operator contacted the command post in Egypt on his satellite link. Told of clear skies at Desert One, Seiffert decided to continue.

Meanwhile, Dash 3, 4, and 5 moved closer together to keep one another in sight and flew on. Dash 7 and 8 brought up the rear, separated from each other and from the helicopters now ahead of them. Cockpit temperatures climbed to ninety-three degrees in the blinding dust, and the parched pilots called to their crew chiefs for water. In Dash 3, Major Jim Schaefer slowed the three-ship formation to ninety knots and began climbing to clear a 6,000-foot mountain ahead. At 5,900 feet, the dust thinned enough for him to spot the mountain off to his left. Then he plunged into a second haboob. Somewhere ahead lay a 9,000-foot mountain. Again visibility improved, and he saw the mountain slip by on his left. He had been in the dust for almost three hours. He was thirty-five minutes away from Desert One and overdue.

Schaefer could count himself lucky. In Dash 5, Lieutenant Rod Davis, the last of the Navy pilots, was in real trouble. An electrical power supply had overheated and failed. With the electricity went the chopper's artificial horizon and several other navigation aids. Having neither a real horizon to look at outside nor an artificial one on the instrument panel, any pilot is apt to develop vertigo, as Davis did. Before he could pass control to his copilot, the chopper had slipped into a forty-degree bank. Leveling the helicopter, the copilot descended to seventy-five feet; the better view of the ground from that height helped deter the disorientation that Davis had

This flight plan, found in one of the abandoned Sea Stallions and published in Iran, details the route from the *Nimitz* to Desert One and on to the hide site, or laager. The left column shows the route by turning point, starting with the ship and the coast-in point (CIP), where the helicopters crossed the coast. The other columns show landmarks for turning points, the course in degrees for each leg of the flight, the length of each leg in nautical miles, flying speed, the flying time in minutes for each segment, as well as the hour in Greenwich Mean Time, elapsed time in hours and minutes, and coordinates for turning points.

154

experienced. The aircraft's radiomagnetic compass and flight-control computer had also fallen victim to the power outage. In this condition, Davis's helicopter had become unfit to perform the rest of its mission. Davis briefly broke radio silence to announce his decision to abort, then reversed course for the *Nimitz*. He barely made it. When he arrived, he had almost run out of fuel.

Schaefer in Dash 3 reached Desert One first—fifty minutes late. He landed, taxied to his assigned C-130 for refueling, and climbed exhausted from the cockpit. Beckwith stalked over, demanding to know where the rest of the choppers were. "They're either coming," said Schaefer, wearily, "or they're up against the side of a hill." Then he told of the haboobs.

The remaining five helicopters straggled in over the next thirty-five minutes, almost an hour and a half late. Even if the refueling proceeded without a hitch, Delta could not get to the hide site near Tehran before dawn. The helicopter crews had brought along decals that they could stick on the choppers to make them look like Iranian aircraft to a casual observer. Even so, things could get very sticky if the Iranians spotted the helicopters. True to his nickname, Chargin' Charlie had already made his decision: "No matter when the choppers arrived—and no matter when we arrived at the hide site—we would go ahead."

As the Sea Stallions refueled and Delta began to board, Lieutenant Colonel Seiffert climbed down from Dash 1. Visiting each of the pilots, he discovered another problem: Captain B. J. McGuire in Dash 2 confirmed what his instruments had been indicating for the past two hours. The helicopter's primary hydraulic system had failed. A leak in the line had bled the system dry, and the pump had burned out. He could fly—as he had been—on the backup system, but if it failed, a crash was certain. McGuire, a gutsy young aviator, wanted to go on. "No problem," he said. But Seiffert vetoed the idea.

There were now only five flyable choppers at Desert One, one fewer than needed. Mission rules stipulated cancellation. Air boss Kyle radioed Vaught at Wadi Qena. Vaught said to ask Beckwith if he thought he could continue.

All the aircraft engines had been left running to preclude restarting difficulties. In the swirling dust, amid the howl of C-130 and RH-53D turbines, Charlie Beckwith faced a serious decision. Even with six machines, the helicopters were each 6,000 pounds overweight. With only five aircraft, he would have to leave twenty men behind—but which twenty? He thought: "In a tight mission, no one is expendable even before you begin." All the meticulous planning would be shot to hell. And what if another, or even two more machines gave out? How would he extract Delta and the hostages? A bloodbath, a slaughter, could result. The mission was to save Americans, not get them killed along with hundreds of Iranians. He turned to Kyle. "Ain't no way, Jim. No way," Beckwith shouted. "You tell me which of those 130s you want me to load up. Delta's going home."

Monitoring his satellite radio at the hide site near Tehran, Dick Meadows heard from the command post at Wadi Qena: "Spare parts will not arrive due to broken truck. Test canceled." Incredulous, Meadows requested clarification. Vaught broke in on the circuit: "Close test base Romeo," he ordered peremptorily. Meadows, his Air Force sergeant, and the Green Berets returned to Tehran. In the next few days, all but one would slip out of Iran. Fred, fluent in Farsi, stayed behind to ensure that everyone else was safely away.

At Desert One, the force began deplaning from the helicopters and filing onto the C-130s. Beckwith went from one plane to another, working out how many men would load onto each one of the C-130s and worrying that the pilots might take off without them. "For God's sake, don't leave," he yelled to one aviator. "Ain't nobody going to leave here, Colonel, until we got everybody," shouted back the pilot.

The C-130s had been on the ground for nearly three hours, with their engines running the entire time. If the C-130 carrying Delta's Blue team did not take off within five minutes, it could not reach Masirah Island without tanker assistance. But before the C-130

A paean to freedom, in both English and Farsi, decorates an American flag intended to be hoisted at the American embassy in Tehran as the rescue force pulled out after liberating the hostages. The Farsi translation was provided by the Iranian-born U.S. Air Force sergeant who, as Fred, accompanied Dick Meadows on his premission reconnaissance of Tehran.

THIS FLAG IS DEDICATED TO FREEDOM: AN IDEAL AMERICANS WILL NEVER FORGET AND OPPRESSORS WILL NEVER UNDERSTAND.

could taxi, Jim Schaefer had to move Dash 3 from its parking spot behind the transport. The prop wash from the C-130 as it increased power would stir up enough dust to choke the chopper's engines. Schaefer could not just taxi out of the way; a tire had come off its rim as the chopper crossed a furrow in the sand left by one of the C-130s. He would have to lift off and reposition.

Visibility at Desert One had become almost as bad as in the haboobs. Even at idle power, the churning helicopter rotors and the C-130 turboprops kicked up small tornadoes of dust. As Schaefer increased the pitch of the rotor blades, they bit into the Iranian night air, lifting the helicopter into a hover. An Air Force combat controller stood nearby as a reference point for the pilot.

Perhaps it was fatigue from the flight through the haboobs. Perhaps it was a psychological low, now that the mission had been scrubbed. Whatever the cause, to Schaefer, watching through night-vision goggles, the controller appeared to back to the left, a sign that the helicopter was drifting to the right. Schaefer's misinterpretation caused him to make a fatal adjustment—toward the C-130.

"I felt a shudder and felt two thunks," recalled Logan Fitch, Blue element commander sitting inside the transport. He and his men scrambled for the right-side door, the only one not instantly curtained in flames. By some miracle, they and aircrew members in the back of the plane all escaped. Of the seven men on the flight deck, two were blown clear by explosions; the rest perished.

The planning and execution were too incompetent to believe," snorted one Israeli officer.

Aboard the helicopter, Schaefer's copilot climbed out a window and dashed away through a puddle of fuel, as yet unignited. Schaefer feared—without cause—that the intense heat in the cockpit might set off the bullets in his .45 automatic. He shrugged out of his shoulder holster, unbuckled his safety harness, and dived from the cockpit, cracking two vertebrae as his head hit the ground. Someone picked him up and helped him to a C-130. The rest of his crew burned to death.

Ammunition aboard the C-130 and the chopper started cooking off. Redeye antiaircraft missiles pinwheeled through the air, and shrapnel spattered the closest helicopters. A short distance away, Kyle, in communication with Egypt, turned and asked Beckwith about the helicopters. Beckwith said that the heat could explode a second helicopter any second. They decided to abandon the Sea Stallions, load the crews onto the C-130s, and fly out of there. Kyle called Vaught for an air strike to destroy the choppers left behind, then he and Beckwith walked to the last C-130.

It was almost 3:00 a.m. Delta had been on the ground four hours and fifty-six minutes. Eight men lay dead and some $72 million worth of equipment had been lost or destroyed. Operation Rice Bowl was over before it had fairly begun.

No one said much of anything on the flight back to Wadi Qena. Beckwith sat alone thinking, "Jesus Christ. What a mess. We've just embarrassed our great country." There was more. In Egypt, Beckwith learned that the air strike had not been sent in to destroy the helicopters, for fear of endangering the Iranian bus passengers. Iran had five Sea Stallions—along with a propaganda windfall. The danger of explosion had argued against sanitizing two of the RH-53Ds of classified documents—flight plans, the hide-site location, and other details of the mission.

On the afternoon of April 28, after Delta Force had returned to Camp Smokey, President Carter paid a visit. He embraced Beckwith and shook every man's hand, speaking with each one for a minute or longer. Before departing, he told Beckwith: "I didn't know we still had people like this, people who would sacrifice everything for their country. Colonel, I am very proud of these men." The president later said that Beckwith had wept, and confessed that he had, too.

Carter then gave the order to plan a second mission, Operation Snow Bird. Preparations went on in great secrecy for several months, and the force grew larger than the one for Rice Bowl. But the operation was never launched, because the hostages could never be pinpointed. In twos and threes, they had been secretly moved out of the embassy compound and scattered throughout the country.

Meanwhile, the Iranians burned more U.S. flags. In time, the dead Marines and Air Force men were returned to the United States, and no harm came to the hostages. The Soviet Union feigned outrage, while America's allies offered commiseration. A British brigadier with SAS experience called it "the most difficult military rescue attempt in history." But not everyone responded so generously. "The planning and execution were too incompetent to believe," snorted one Israeli officer.

The Americans failed so completely that many at home tended to agree with the Israeli. Every journalist offered a postmortem; scathing books appeared. Congress investigated, and the Joint Chiefs empaneled a blue-ribbon Special Operations Review Group of six senior officers to examine every aspect of the mission.

Many questions arose—about the choice of pilots, about the number of helicopters, about the stringent OPSEC, about training and rehearsals, about too-strict observance of radio silence. A list of topics examined by the review group ran to nearly twenty items. There were answers, some good, some not so good, to all the questions. The review group, though critical of some of the choices made and decisions reached, could not identify a fatal error that had doomed the mission. An additional helicopter or two probably would have allowed Rice Bowl to proceed beyond Desert One. However, because of the delays caused by the haboobs, Delta Force would have arrived at the hide site after dawn regardless of how many helicopters had participated. Had the forecasting of haboobs been possible, the mission might have been postponed until the next night.

At a Senate hearing, Georgia's Sam Nunn, chairman of the Armed Services Committee, asked Colonel Beckwith what he had learned from the Rice Bowl mission and how to preclude such failures in the future. Beckwith began by stating that Murphy's Law applies to all endeavors: If something can go wrong, it will go wrong. "Murphy's in every drawer, under every rock, on top of every hill. Sir, we purely had bad luck."

Then Beckwith answered the second part of the question. "If Coach Bear Bryant at the University of Alabama put his quarterback in Virginia, his backfield in North Carolina, his offensive line in Georgia, and his defense in Texas and then got Delta Airlines to pick them up and fly them to Birmingham on game day, he wouldn't have his winning teams."

The colonel continued: "In Iran we had an ad hoc affair. We went out, found bits and pieces, people and equipment, brought them together occasionally, and then asked them to perform a highly complex mission. The parts all performed, but they didn't necessarily perform as a team."

Finally, Beckwith said: "My recommendation is to put together an organization that contains everything it will ever need, an organization that would include Delta, the Rangers, the Navy SEALs, Air Force pilots, its own staff, its own support people, its own aircraft and helicopters. Make this organization a permanent military unit. Allocate sufficient funds. And give it sufficient time to recruit, assess, and train its people."

That was the nub of it. After hundreds of interviews, numerous visits to units, and much deliberation, the Joint Chiefs' Special Operations Review Group arrived at approximately the same conclusion. The chairman, retired admiral James L. Holloway, wrote of the Iran rescue mission: "Only the United States military, alone in the world, had the ability to accomplish what we set out to do. The final plan offered the best chance of success, and the people were the

An Iranian soldier stands guard near a propeller stuck into the Iranian desert, a grim symbol of the failed attempt to free Americans held hostage in Tehran. The wreckage is all that remained of a C-130 and the helicopter that collided with it as the rescue force was about to depart from Desert One.

Charred areas in the inset at left are helicopters destroyed in air strikes mounted by Iranian F-4 fighters against the five abandoned aircraft. Flown two days after the catastrophe, the purpose of the air strikes may have been to guarantee that the Americans would not return for the choppers.

finest. They deserved to succeed. The trouble was that a fully trained and integrated force was not available from the outset." Holloway's group recommended that "a Counterterrorist Joint Task Force be established as a permanent field agency of the Joint Chiefs of Staff with permanently assigned staff personnel and certain assigned forces."

Some time later, Charlie Beckwith learned that he was to be reassigned. The Joint Chiefs had approved a Special Operations Command much as he had suggested to Senator Sam Nunn and as the Holloway group had recommended. It would operate independently of the individual military services and would report directly to the Joint Chiefs. It would have its own forces and be able to call on other services for additional assets. Colonel Beckwith was to help work out the details. After more frustration, Charlie Beckwith retired from the Army to run a security service that he named, with evident irony, SAS of Texas.

Since the debacle at Desert One, the United States' special forces have been considerably expanded and thoroughly reorganized. By 1987, all special-operations forces had been gathered under one umbrella, the Assistant Secretary of Defense for Special Operations and Low-Intensity Conflict. At the operational level, jurisdiction over the special-operations units themselves has been assumed by an independent United States Special Operations Command (USSOCOM), one of eight combatant administrations in the U.S. military. Located at MacDill Air Force Base in Tampa, Florida, USSOCOM is headed by a full general, who reports directly to the Joint Chiefs of Staff.

From a relatively meager budget of $400 million annually, funding for special-operations forces climbed to $3.2 billion in the 1990 budget, a figure that could become even larger in future budgets despite the enthusiasms for lowering the defense budget in the light of reduced tension between East and West. This money is meant to buy a special-operations structure approaching 35,000 regulars and reserves outfitted with some of the most sophisticated equipment in the U.S. inventory.

However, all the equipment imaginable will not make much difference without sufficient funds to keep it in operating condition. Larger numbers of special-operations slots will have little effect if enough qualified soldiers cannot be found to fill them. And additional men are of little use if equipment purchases consume so much money that training must be curtailed.

Such issues are of genuine concern. Troops that may have to act on short notice need to be primed to go, but for much of the 1980s, they were only marginally mission-capable. "Readiness," acknowledges one Pentagon official, "has been atrocious." On a scale from C1 (fully ready) to C4 (not ready), most units scored only C3 (ready with substantial deficiencies). The inadequacies ranged from too few airplanes in working condition and a low level of foreign-language proficiency to problems recruiting medics. As the 1980s came to a close, the SEALs and some Air Force units achieved a C2 readiness level. Delta Force has also maintained a C2 rating, but most Army special-operations units still struggle along at C3.

Underlying these shortcomings may be that special operations remain a little-loved stepchild within the Pentagon. The attitude is a matter of both culture and perception. In its own way, the U.S. military reflects the egalitarian society that it is sworn to protect, and unorthodox elite units have always been regarded with suspicion, even distaste.

Yet, in an era when there seems to be only a remote chance of a war that would require the full weight of the United States' jet fighters and bombers, its tanks, artillery, and infantry, its aircraft carriers and nuclear submarines, special-operations forces may stand the best chance of seeing action. They would almost certainly play an important role in any future operations such as Just Cause in Panama. The Special Forces, echoing their role in Vietnam, have trained soldiers in El Salvador and other Central American countries, and other nations have appealed for their assistance. American citizens remain vulnerable in a world where the taking of hundreds of hostages is seen by some governments as a defensible tool of foreign policy. Add to these possibilities the revival in Europe and elsewhere of old animosities that until recent years had been suppressed by the iron grip of the Soviet Union, and the need for a competent U.S. special-operations capability may never have been greater. That much was clear to Secretary of State George Shultz in 1986. "Low-intensity conflict," he said, "is the prime challenge we will face, at least through the remainder of this century. The future of peace and freedom may well depend on how effectively we meet it." ★★★★

A Supercopter for
Rigorous Missions

In a volatile world plagued by flash-fire conflicts and hostage taking, special-operations teams must be able to move swiftly and secretly to the roughest and most remote parts of the globe. Often the only way to accomplish that is to travel by helicopter—and the U.S. Air Force's hulking MH-53J, shown here, is unquestionably the most sophisticated machine for the purpose on earth.

Known as the Pave Low III helicopter, the MH-53J is basically the same workhorse machine that was known in Vietnam as the Super Jolly Green Giant. But it is now loaded with an impressive array of infrared sensors, multiple radars, inertial navigation systems, and other electronic gear that enable pilots to fly missions of staggering complexity. Flying at night and at low altitude to foil detection, the Pave Lows can race at 200 mph over virtually any terrain at levels of 100 feet or less, avoiding all obstacles. They can find their way unerringly to any point on the globe. Once at their destination, they can hover automatically at exactly the right height and position to insert special-operations forces, extract them afterward, or rescue others who become stranded in enemy territory.

The need for such a supercopter became obvious in Vietnam—where existing choppers could retrieve men only by day—then became urgent when helicopters trying to rescue hostages from Iran in 1980 proved inadequate *(Chapter 4)*. The MH-53J meets the need: It can go nearly anyplace under almost any conditions and—since it can refuel in flight—it can tackle missions hundreds of miles away.

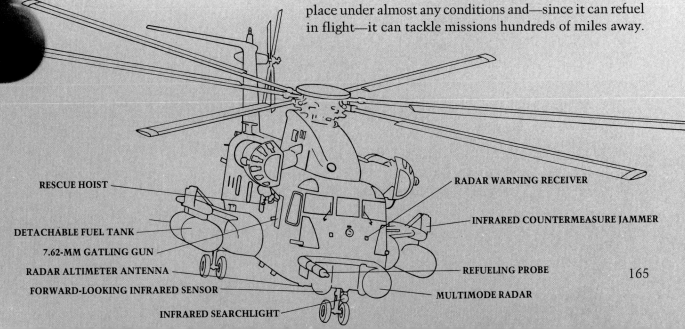

RESCUE HOIST

RADAR WARNING RECEIVER

DETACHABLE FUEL TANK

INFRARED COUNTERMEASURE JAMMER

7.62-MM GATLING GUN

RADAR ALTIMETER ANTENNA

REFUELING PROBE

FORWARD-LOOKING INFRARED SENSOR

MULTIMODE RADAR

INFRARED SEARCHLIGHT

Three instruments crucial to all-weather insertions and extractions, night or day, are built into the Pave Low cockpit, shown here both in daylight *(right)* and lighted with a dull glow that does not interfere with a pilot's view of objects outside the cockpit through night-vision goggles *(above)*. At far left in the picture is a display screen for the terrain-following/terrain-avoidance radar. In flight, it shows obstacles in the helicopter's path; the green blob in the inset, for example, represents a mountain ahead. Just to the right of the radar is the FLIR screen. In addition to an image of the landscape in the helicopter's flight path, the screen has a horizon bar that shows whether the aircraft is in level flight, as well as other readouts that show flight direction, groundspeed, and altitude. To the right of the FLIR and below it is the moving map display. In the mode of operation shown here, the helicopter is located at the bottom of the V-shape on the screen.

Piercing the Blackness
with Electronic Eyes

As Pave Low pilots hustle along on a night-time low-altitude mission they have one crucial need. They must somehow get a picture of the terrain ahead—the hills, trees, bridges, power lines, and other obstructions that could cause a fatal crash. Their basic tools are special night-vision goggles that help the pilots' eyes pierce the darkness by amplifying light from moon or stars.

More vital still are two electronic devices that let the pilots view the upcoming terrain when they cannot see it because of bad weather. The first is a forward-looking infrared sensor (FLIR), which picks up heat from objects, then projects a video-like image of them on a cockpit monitor. The second magical instrument is, in military jargon, a "terrain-following/terrain-avoidance radar," which not only provides another picture of what lies ahead but also warns the pilots when to pull up and fly over an obstacle or go around it. Both are backed up by a moving map display that shows exactly where the MH-53J is at every instant along its projected flight path.

An aerial minuet. For air-to-air refueling, a C-130 flies over and
past the MH-53J *(upper arrow)*,
then maintains altitude and
slows to about 120 mph—the
minimum safe speed for a fully
loaded tanker. The helicopter
pilots, seeing the plane in front
and above them, creep forward

move closer, they carefully aim
their fuel probe at the hose and
drogue the C-130 has unreeled.
The hose extends eighty feet
from a wing tank, as shown, so
the copter will not have to fly
through the center of the plane's

finished, the helicopter slowly
reduces speed, probe and drogue
uncoupling automatically. The
tanker resumes its normal cruis

The Hairsbreadth Art of Air-to-Air Refueling

Among the many nerve-racking elements of a low-flying night mission in an MH-53J is the touch-and-go maneuver shown at left: refueling in the dark while cruising a few perilous feet from the belly of a blacked-out C-130 tanker. The helicopter, even with detachable auxiliary fuel tanks, has a maximum range of 750 miles. If called upon to penetrate deep within hostile air space, a crew might need to rendezvous with tankers two or three times—both on the way in and on the flight home.

To prepare for refueling, the C-130 proceeds to a prearranged rendezvous with the helicopter. As the MH-53J approaches at a lower altitude, its position is revealed to the tanker's crew on radar and by signal lights mounted on top of the helicopter's rotor blades. The C-130 flies in over the Pave Low, as shown in the diagram at bottom left, and extends a fuel line tipped by a basketlike drogue *(near left)*. The helicopter pilots must then maneuver a 16-foot-long fuel probe into the drogue—and hold it there for up to ten minutes while fuel is transferred from tanker to chopper. "A lot of helicopter pilots are just truck drivers," one 20th Squadron veteran jokes, "but when you're flying an MH-53J you're skilled labor."

An aiming point. Trailing at the end of a refueling hose, a cone-shaped drogue gives the helicopter crew a target for the fuel probe. The drogue also acts as a stabilizer for the fuel line. At its apex is a coupling device that clamps onto the probe to form a sealed connection with the fuel line.

169

At the Target Zone, a Magic-Carpet Ride

Even after tree-hopping hundreds of miles through darkness—and sometimes bad weather—the pilots of an MH-53J still have some of their trickiest work to do: get the troops riding in the helicopter's cargo hold neatly and quickly on the ground. If terrain, weather, and situation allow, the pilots may land. More often they hover, so the men can rapidly slide down ropes to the ground like firemen down a pole *(far left)*.

Crucial to this exercise is a stable hover, one of the most difficult tasks in aviation under the best of circumstances. It is unachievable even by a skilled pilot when darkness or bad weather obscures ground and horizon, making it impossible for him to tell whether the aircraft is stationary.

The remedy is a remarkable device called a hover coupler, which processes signals from gyroscopes, a radar altimeter, and the helicopter's inertial guidance system to keep the chopper hovering steadily *(diagrams, left)*. Engaged when the chopper is about one minute away from its destination, the hover coupler nurses the aircraft the final few miles of the journey and stops it at a preselected altitude, usually about forty feet, directly above a preprogrammed point on the ground. Then the coupler holds the helicopter steady.

The MH-53J's capabilities have been repeatedly tested in practice—and with remarkable success. In one exercise, MH-53J crews brought in seven helicopters exactly on target within two seconds of target time after a seven-and-a-half-hour flight and four in-flight refuelings—and landed thirty men each in five seconds.

Countering pitch and roll. To keep an MH-53J on an even keel, the hover coupler *(red dot, above)* employs gyroscopes in the rear of the helicopter *(blue dots)* to sense when the nose rises or falls or when the helicopter rolls to one side or the other. Signals from the gyros are processed by the coupler, which issues electronic instructions to the rotor hub, which adjusts the pitch of the blades to correct the problem.

Controlling yaw. Other gyroscopes in the front of the Pave Low helicopter send impulses that tell the hover coupler if the aircraft changes heading. Then the coupler changes the pitch of the tail rotor blades to keep the chopper's nose pointed in the right direction.

Maintaining altitude. A radar altimeter, which gauges height by measuring the split second a radar impulse requires to reach the ground and bounce back, produces the signals that hold a hovering MH-53J at a constant altitude. Digesting the signals, the hover coupler sends messages to the rotor control, which regulates the pitch of the rotor blades to counteract updrafts, downdrafts, and even the change in weight as troops exit.

Acknowledgments

The editors wish to thank Guy Aceto, *Air Force*, Arlington, Va.; Edwin Alber, Olin Corp., East Alton, Ill.; Col. Arthur Andraitis (Ret.), Oakton, Va.; Lt. Col. Joseph Argentieri, Ft. Bragg, N.C.; Jonathan Arms, Arms Communications, Woodbridge, Va.; Tim Bagniefski, Olin Corp., East Alton, Ill.; Col. Charlie A. Beckwith (Ret.), Austin, Tex.; Dale D. Brinkman, Robins AFB, Ga.; James W. Canan, *Air Force*, Arlington, Va.; Véronique Cardineaux, Paris; Ken Carter, Office of Secretary of Defense Public Affairs, Pentagon; Francesco Cito, Milan; Norval Clinebell, Mesa, Ariz.; CW3 James Combs, Ft. Bragg; Lt. Col. Richard L. Comer, Hurlburt Field, Fla.; Joseph E. Dabney, Lockheed Aeronautical Systems, Marietta, Ga.; Mavis T. Dezulovich, Ft. Belvoir, Va.; Col. John W. Dye, MacDill AFB, Tampa, Fla.; Russell Egnor, USN, Pentagon; Lt. Col. David Eshel (Ret.), Israel Army, Hod Hasharon, Israel; Col. Art Forster, USAF, Pentagon; Fred Fuller, Marquat Memorial Library, Ft. Bragg; Robert Edison Fulton, Jr., Newtown, Conn.; Steve Galloway, Heckler & Koch, Chantilly, Va.; Lt. Col. Jack Garrison, USAF, Springfield, Va.; Michael T. Gartman, IBM, Owego, N.Y.; Lt. Col. Doneal Gersh, Ft. Bragg; Vernon Gillespie, Arlington, Va.; Katja Gloger, *Stern*, Hamburg; Alan Golacinsky, Global Strategies Group, Washington; Col. George Gray, Hurlburt Field; Nancy G. Greer, Texas Instruments, Dallas; Stephen Grimes, London; Col. James G. "Bo" Gritz, Sandy Valley, Nev.; Col. Roland D. Guidry (Ret.), Shalimar, Fla.; Frank Hackley, Gen Corp Aerojet Ordnance, Downey, Calif.; Hans Halberstadt, San Jose, Calif.; Victoria Hanson, Spangdahlem Air Base, Germany; Lt. Col. Darrell C. Hayes, USAF, Pentagon; Lynn Helmintoller, Hurlburt Field; Gregory Hendrix, Department of Defense Still Media Records Center, Washington; Philip Karber, Great Falls, Va.; Helen A. Kavanaugh, Wright-Patterson AFB, Ohio; Harvey Keene, USA, Natick, Mass.; Lt. Doug Kinneard, Hurlburt Field; Pat Laney, Varo, Inc., Garland, Tex.; Robert E. Leiendecker, Charlottesville, Va.; CSM Joseph Lupyak (Ret.), Ft. Bragg; Maj. Ken McGraw, Ft. Bragg; Ken MacKenzie, Paris; Jean-Pierre Maldonado, Litton Electron Tube Division, Tempe, Ariz.; William T. Markey, Ft. Belvoir; Capt. Richard J. Meadows (Ret.), Crestview, Fla.; Roxanne Merritt, JFK Special Warfare Museum, Ft. Bragg; Mark Meyer, Smyrna, Del.; Cmdr. Steven Moore, Ft. Bragg; SGM Joseph Murray, Ft. Bragg; Lt. Col. B. B. Napier, Hurlburt Field; George Neranchi, Defense Technology, Los Altos, Calif.; Michael O'Leary, Challenge Publications, Canoga Park, Calif.; Sylvie Papillon, Direction Generale de l'Armement, Paris; Fred Pickler, AAI Corp., Hunt Valley, Md.; Marina Ponzio, Lucky Star, Milan; Betty Ponzone, Albatross Press Agency, Milan; William Rosenmund, USA, Pentagon; Col. James H. Schaefer, USMC, Washington; Col. Edward R. Seiffert, USMC, Quantico, Va.; Eric Shulzinger, Lockheed Aeronautical Systems, Burbank, Calif.; Maj. Phil Soucy, USA, Pentagon; Bettie E. Sprigg, Office of Secretary of Defense Public Affairs, Pentagon; Jerry Steelman, *Special Warfare*, Ft. Bragg; Thomas F. Swearengen, Burton, S.C.; Bill Taylor, Aberdeen Proving Ground, Md.; Patricia Toombs, USN, Pentagon; Lt. Col. Francis P. Tunstall, Jr., USAF, Pentagon; Lt. Gen. James B. Vaught (Ret.), Mt. Pleasant, S.C.; Robert A. Waller, Jr., Department of Defense Still Media Records Center, Washington; Joseph J. Wiedmann, Ft. Belvoir; Capt. Claudia R. Ziebas, Hurlburt Field.

Bibliography

BOOKS

Adams, James, *Secret Armies: Inside the American, Soviet and European Special Forces*. New York: Atlantic Monthly Press, 1988.

Beckwith, Col. Charlie A., USA (Ret.), and Donald Knox, *Delta Force*. New York: Harcourt Brace Jovanovich, 1983.

Bonds, Ray, ed., *The World's Elite Forces*. London: Salamander Books, 1987.

Burgess, William, ed., *Inside Spetsnaz*. Novato, Calif.: Presidio Press, 1989.

Cacutt, Len, ed., *Combat*. Secaucus, N.J.: Chartwell Books, 1988.

David, Heather, *Operation: Rescue*. New York: Pinnacle Books, 1971.

Donahue, James C., *No Greater Love: A Day with the Mobile Guerrilla Force in Vietnam*. Canton, Ohio: Daring Books, 1988.

Emerson, Steven, *Secret Warriors: Inside the Covert Military Operations of the Reagan Era*. New York: G. P. Putnam's Sons, 1988.

Ezell, Edward Clinton, *The AK47 Story*. Harrisburg, Pa.: Stackpole Books, 1988.

Garrett, Richard, *The Raiders*. New York: Van Nostrand Reinhold, 1980.

Geraghty, Tony, *Inside the Special Air Service*. Nashville: Battery Press, 1980.

Halberstadt, Hans, *Green Berets: Unconventional Warriors*. Novato, Calif.: Presidio Press, 1988.

Hogg, Ian V., and John Weeks, *Military Small Arms of the 20th Century*. Northfield, Ill.: DBI Books, 1985.

Kelly, Col. Francis J., *U.S. Army Special Forces 1961-1971*. Washington: Dept. of the Army, 1973.

Kennedy, Michael Paul, *Soldier 'I' S.A.S.* London: Bloomsbury Publishing, 1989.

Macdonald, Peter, *The Special Forces*. Secaucus, N.J.: Chartwell Books, 1987.

Maitland, Terrence, Stephen Weiss, and the Editors of Boston Publishing, *Raising the Stakes* (The Vietnam Experience series). Boston Publishing, 1982.

Markham, George, *Guns of the Elite*. Dorset, England: Arms and Armour Press, 1987.

Palmer, Terry, *Discover The Gambia*. Clacton-on-Sea, England: Heritage House, 1989.

Ryan, Paul B., *The Iranian Rescue Mission: Why It Failed*. Annapolis: Naval Institute Press, 1985.

Schemmer, Benjamin F., *The Raid*. New York: Avon Books, 1986.

Stanton, Shelby L., *Green Berets at War: U.S. Army Special Forces in Southeast Asia 1956-1975*. Novato, Calif.: Presidio Press, 1985.

Swearengen, Thomas F., *The World's Fighting Shotguns*. Alexandria, Va.: T.B.N. Enterprises, 1978.

Westmoreland, Gen. William C., *A Soldier Reports*. New York: Doubleday, 1976.

PERIODICALS

Beecher, William, "U.S. Rescue Force Landed within 23 Miles of Hanoi, but It Found P.O.W.'s Gone." *New York Times*, Nov. 24, 1970.

Bird, Julie, "Pave Low Crews Thrive on Danger, Excitement." *Air Force Times*, June 26, 1989.

"Blackmailing the U.S." *Time*, Nov. 19, 1979.

Braestrup, Peter, "Behind the Training for Viet Raid: Scale Model of Camp, Tight Secrecy." *Washington Post*, Nov. 27, 1970.

Bulloch, John, "SAS Free Family of Ruler: Gambian Rebels Disarmed." *Daily Telegraph* (London), Aug. 7, 1981.

Burns, John, and James Davies, "Maggie Orders SAS to Rescue." *Daily Express* (London), Aug. 7, 1981.

Butler, David, et al., "A Helpless Giant in Iran." *Newsweek*, Nov. 19, 1979.

Chapman, William, "The Sontay Story." *Washing-*

ton Post, Nov. 29, 1970.
Colucci, Frank:
· "Stronger SOF." *Defence Helicopter World*, Jan. 1989.
"Target Hind!" *Defence Helicopter World*, Mar. 1989.
"Daring Raids in Vietnam: Purpose of Nixon's Move." *U.S. News & World Report*, Dec. 7, 1970.
Dash, Leon, "Gambia's Democracy Has a Tighter Grip." *Washington Post*, June 6, 1983.
Deac, Wilfred P., "Sky Train Invasion." *Modern Warfare*, July 1989.
Dobbie, Peter, "How the SAS Freed Tourists." *Sunday Telegraph* (London), Aug. 9, 1981.
Duodu, Cameron, "Gambians 'Would Not Shoot Whites.' " *Sunday Times* (London), Aug. 9, 1981.
Earl, Maj. Robert L., USMC, "A Matter of Principle." *U.S. Naval Institute Proceedings* (Annapolis, Md.), Feb. 1983.
Farrar, Fred, "Volunteer Force Hits Near Hanoi." *Chicago Tribune*, Nov. 24, 1970.
Fishman, Steve, "Gambia: Tiny Sliver of a Country Still Shaking after Coup Attempt." *Christian Science Monitor*, Aug. 14, 1981.
Fuller, John, "A Lesson From History: The Son Tay Raid." *Observer* (Scott Air Force Base, Ill.), Nov. 1984.
"Gambia Rebels Call on Senegal to Move Troops." *New York Times*, Aug. 1, 1981.
Getler, Michael:
"Mission." *Washington Post*, Nov. 25, 1970.
"Raid." *Washington Post*, Nov. 28, 1970.
Green, Lt. Steve, "Naval Special Warfare: From Frogmen to SEALs." *Special Warfare* (Washington: GPO), Spring 1989.
"Hanoi's Pawns: The U.S. Prisoners of War." *Newsweek*, Nov. 30, 1970.
Harris, Richard, "Raid at Son Tay." *American History Illustrated*, Apr. 1990.
Hersh, Seymour M., "Intelligence Called Faulty in Viet Prison Camp Raid." *Baltimore Sun*, Jan. 29, 1971.
"Iran: The Test of Wills." *Time*, Nov. 26, 1979.
Lewis, Jay, "Charles Beckwith: Two Years After the Raid on Iran." *Dallas Times Herald*, May 30, 1982.
Loory, Stuart H., "The Problem of Intelligence: Story behind Raid on Son Tay Prison." *Los Angeles Times*, Feb. 2, 1971.
Marder, Murrey, "U.S. Claims 'Net Plus' for Raid." *Washington Post*, Nov. 29, 1970.
Martin, David C., "Inside the Rescue Mission." *Newsweek*, July 12, 1982.
"Matchet's Diary." *West Africa*, Aug. 17, 1981.
"Murder in the Mountains: A Bloody Coup Rattles a Shaky, Strife-Torn Soviet Satellite." *Time*, Oct. 1, 1979.
"A New Cold War." *Newsweek*, Jan. 14, 1980.

Ondrasik, Barbara, "The Prison Raid Raised Hopes. . . ." *New York Times*, Dec. 8, 1970.
"Operation Successful, Results Nil." *Newsweek*, Dec. 7, 1970.
Pines, Burton, "How the Soviet Army Crushed Afghanistan." *Time*, Jan. 14, 1980.
Rhodes, Jeffrey P.:
"Any Time Any Place." *Air Force Magazine*, June 1988.
"The Machines of Special Ops." *Air Force Magazine*, Aug. 1988.
Ruhl, Robert K., "Raid at Son Tay." *Airman*, Aug. 1975.
"SAS Helps to Free Gambia Hostages." *Times* (London), Aug. 7, 1981.
Sochurer, Howard, "Americans in Action in Viet Nam." *National Geographic*, Jan. 1965.
"Special Forces." *Flight International*, Sept. 10, 1988.
Szilagyi, Pete, "Always a Soldier at Heart: Hero of Rescue Try Settles in New Job." *American Statesman* (Austin, Tex.), Nov. 8, 1981.
"23rd Air Force: Special Operations in the Air." *Special Warfare* (Washington: GPO), Spring 1989.
Wilson, George C., "Sontay: Shots, Shouts, Sinking Feeling." *Washington Post*, Dec. 10, 1970.

OTHER SOURCES
"Pave Low III Enhanced MH-53J Roll-Out." Brochure. Pensacola, Fla.: Naval Aviation Depot, July 17, 1987.
"Text of Pentagon News Conference on U.S. Rescue Mission into North Vietnam." *New York Times*, Nov. 24, 1970.
U.S. Congress. House. Committee on Foreign Affairs. *Iran's Seizure of the United States Embassy.* 97th Cong. 1st sess., Feb. 17-Mar. 11, 1981. Committee Print. Washington: GPO, 1981.
U.S. Congress. Senate. Committee on Foreign Relations. *Bombing Operations and the Prisoner-of-War Rescue Mission in North Vietnam.* 91st Cong. 2d sess., with Melvin R. Laird, Secretary of Defense, Nov. 24, 1970. Committee Print. Washington: GPO, 1971.
U.S. Joint Chiefs of Staff, *Holloway Commission Report.* Joint Special Operations Review Group, Aug. 1980.
U.S. Joint Chiefs of Staff, *Operation Kingpin.* Briefing Book for the Joint Chiefs of Staff and National Command Authorities Office. Nov. 1970.
U.S. Joint Chiefs of Staff, *Report on the Son Tay Prisoner of War Rescue Operation.* Parts I and II. Brig. Gen. LeRoy J. Manor, USAF, Commander JCS Joint Contingency Task Group Office, 1971.
Zak, Michael J., "The Iran Hostage Rescue Mission: C3I in the Management of a Project Team." Research draft. Cambridge, Mass.: Harvard University, 1981.

Index

Picture Credits

The sources for the illustrations that appear in this book are listed below. Credits from left to right are separated by semicolons, from top to bottom by dashes.
Initial capital letters throughout the book: Art by Matt McMullen. Cover: Fred J. Maroon. 6: Mark Meyer. 10, 11: Art by Matt McMullen; Mark Meyer. 14, 15: Private Collection. 19: © 1965 Howard Sochurek. 20, 21: JFK Special Warfare Museum, Ft. Bragg, N.C.; © 1965 Howard Sochurek (4). 24: Pictorial Parade; Ken Cooke, courtesy JFK Special Warfare Museum, Ft. Bragg, N.C. 28, 29: Vietnamese News Agency, Hanoi; Library of Congress; AP/Wide World Photos; Art by Hildegard Groves/Med Sci Art Co. 32, 33: U.S. Navy/Department of Defense. 36: James Donahue, courtesy Col. James G. "Bo" Gritz; James Donahue (2). 39: Gary L. Kieffer/Photo Press

International. 40, 41: Fred J. Maroon; Mark Meyer (2)—art by Stephen Wagner. 42, 43: Art by Al Kettler; Mi D. Seitelman/Photo Press International—Art by Bryan Leister (3). 44, 45: Art by Al Kettler; Art by Anthony Wooldridge (3); Gary L. Kieffer/Photo Press International. 46: Mi D. Seitelman/Photo Press International; U.S. Navy/Department of Defense. 47-49: Gary L. Kieffer/Photo Press International. 50, 51: Robert Fulton, Jr. 52, 53: Art by Anthony Wooldridge—Robert Fulton, Jr. 54, 55: Defense Intelligence Agency, courtesy LeRoy Manor. 58, 59: UPI/Bettmann Newsphotos. 62, 63: Simons Collection, JFK Special Warfare Museum, Ft. Bragg, N.C. 67: Art by Fred Holz—U.S. Air Force/Department of Defense. 68, 69: William Patterson, courtesy U.S. Air Force Museum, Wright-Patterson Air Force Base, Ohio. 70, 71: JFK Special

175

Warfare Museum, Ft. Bragg, N.C. 74, 75: Simons Collection, JFK Special Warfare Museum, Ft. Bragg, N.C. 76: Benjamin F. Schemmer Collection, courtesy Armed Forces Journal International. 79: Art by Hildegard Groves/Med Sci Art Co. 80, 81: Art by Kim Barnes/Stansbury, Ronsaville, Wood, Inc. 84: Department of Defense, courtesy Col. Art Andraitis. 86: Romano Cagnoni, Pietrasanta, Italy. 88: Art by Mapping Specialist Ltd. 89: Rick Smolan/Contact Press Images. 91: Rick Smolan, courtesy Woodfin Camp Associates. 92, 93: Hans-Jürgen Burkard/Bilderberg, Hamburg (2). 96, 97: Novosti Press Agency. 98, 99: Hubert Van Es—AP/Wide World Photos. 101: Art by Mapping Specialist Ltd. 102: AP/Wide World Photos. 104, 105: Art by Med Sci Art Co. 106, 107: A.F.P., Paris. 109: Benoit Gysemberg, Camera Press, London. 110, 111: British Library, London. 112-123: Hans Halberstadt/ Arms Communications; art (bullets) by Mark Robinson. 124: U.S. Navy/Department of Defense. 126, 127: Courtesy Research Associates. 129: Roddey E. Mims/TIME. 132, 133: SIPA Press. 134: U.S. Army/Department of Defense. 139: Hans Halberstadt/Arms Communications. 141: Courtesy Research Associates. 145: Lockheed. 146, 147: Mark Meyer. 150, 151: U.S. Navy/Department of Defense. 152, 153: Art by Med Sci Art Co. 154: Courtesy Research Associates. 156, 157: Larry Sherer, courtesy Research Associates. 160, 161: Heikki Kotilainen/Lehtikuva/Photoreporters—Abbas/Magnum. 164, 165: Mark Meyer—art by Mark Robinson. 166, 167: Mark Meyer—U.S. Air Force, courtesy Lt. Col. Rich Comer; Mark Meyer. 168, 169: Mark Meyer (2)—art by Mark Robinson. 170, 171: © 1990 Air Force Times photo by Doug Pensinger; art by Mark Robinson.

TIME ®
LIFE
BOOKS

Time-Life Books Inc.
is a wholly owned subsidiary of
THE TIME INC. BOOK COMPANY

TIME-LIFE BOOKS INC.

MANAGING EDITOR: Thomas H. Flaherty
Director of Editorial Resources: Elise D. Ritter-Clough
Director of Photography and Research:
John Conrad Weiser
Editorial Board: Dale Brown, Roberta Conlan, Laura Foreman, Lee E. Hassig, Jim Hicks, Blaine Marshall, Rita Mullin, Henry Woodhead

PUBLISHER: Joseph J. Ward

Editorial Director: Russell B. Adams, Jr.
Marketing Director: Anne Everhart
Director of Design: Louis Klein
Production Manager: Prue Harris
Supervisor of Quality Control: James King

Editorial Operations
Production: Celia Beattie
Library: Louise D. Forstall
Computer Composition: Deborah G. Tait (Manager), Monika D. Thayer, Janet Barnes Syring, Lillian Daniels

Correspondents: Elisabeth Kraemer-Singh (Bonn), Christine Hinze (London), Christina Lieberman (New York), Maria Vincenza Aloisi (Paris), Ann Natanson (Rome). Valuable assistance was also provided by Elizabeth Brown (New York), Mieko Ikeda (Tokyo), Sasha Isachenko (Moscow), Marlin Levin (Jerusalem), Marguerite Michaels (Nairobi), Felix Rosenthal (Moscow), Nihal Tamraz (Cairo), Ann Wise (Rome), Bing Wong (Hong Kong).

THE NEW FACE OF WAR

SERIES EDITOR: Lee E. Hassig
Series Administrator: Judith W. Shanks

Editorial Staff for *Special Forces and Missions*
Art Director: Christopher M. Register
Picture Editor: Marion F. Briggs
Text Editor: Dale Brown
Associate Editors/Research: Robin Currie, Gwen C. Mullen
Assistant Editors/Research: Ruth Goldberg, Jennifer L. Pearce
Assistant Art Director: Fatima Taylor
Copy Coordinator: Elizabeth Graham
Editorial Assistant: Kathleen S. Walton
Picture Coordinator: Barry Anthony

Special Contributors: Roy Attaway, Clifford Beal, Rita Dallas, George Daniels, Pat Daniels, Jane Ferrell, Jon Guttmann, Thomas Horne, Jerry Korn, John Lang, Rod Paschall, Craig Roberts, Jeremy N. P. Ross, Kathleen Sylvester, David Thomson, C. B. Wismar, Diane Ullius (text); Douglas Brown, John Davidson, Rod Lenahan, Barbara Jones Smith (research); Mel Ingber (index).

Library of Congress Cataloging in Publication Data
Special forces and missions/by the editors of Time-Life Books.
 p. cm. (The New face of war series).
 Includes bibliographical references and index.
 ISBN 0-8094-8600-8
 1. Special operations (Military science). 2. Military history, Modern—20th century. 3. Special forces (Military science).
I. Time-Life Books. II. Series.
U262.S62 1991
355.4—dc20   90-11298 CIP
ISBN 0-8094-8601-6 (lib. bdg.)